OFFICIAL SQA PAST PAPERS WITH ANSWERS

INTERMEDIATE 2

BIOLOGY 2007-2011

SQA

BrightRED PUBLISHING

Publisher's Note

We are delighted to bring you the 2011 Past Papers and you will see that we have changed the format from previous editions. As part of our environmental awareness strategy, we have attempted to make these new editions as sustainable as possible.
To do this, we have printed on white paper and bound the answer sections into the book. This not only allows us to use significantly less paper but we are also, for the first time, able to source all the materials from sustainable sources.

We hope you like the new editions and by purchasing this product, you are not only supporting an independent Scottish publishing company but you are also, in the International Year of Forests, not contributing to the destruction of the world's forests.

Thank you for your support and please see the following websites for more information to support the above statement –

www.fsc-uk.org

www.loveforests.com

First exam published in 2007.
Published by Bright Red Publishing Ltd, 6 Stafford Street, Edinburgh EH3 7AU
tel: 0131 220 5804 fax: 0131 220 6710 info@brightredpublishing.co.uk www.brightredpublishing.co.uk

ISBN 978-1-84948-194-6

A CIP Catalogue record for this book is available from the British Library.

Bright Red Publishing is grateful to the copyright holders, as credited on the final page of the Question Section, for permission to use their material. Every effort has been made to trace the copyright holders and to obtain their permission for the use of copyright material. Bright Red Publishing will be happy to receive information allowing us to rectify any error or omission in future editions.

INTERMEDIATE 2

2007

[BLANK PAGE]

FOR OFFICIAL USE

Total for Sections B and C

X007/201

NATIONAL QUALIFICATIONS 2007

MONDAY, 21 MAY
9.00 AM – 11.00 AM

BIOLOGY INTERMEDIATE 2

Fill in these boxes and read what is printed below.

Full name of centre

Town

Forename(s)

Surname

Date of birth
Day Month Year

Scottish candidate number

Number of seat

SECTION A (25 marks)

Instructions for completion of Section A are given on page two.

For this section of the examination you must use an HB pencil.

SECTIONS B AND C (75 marks)

1 (a) All questions should be attempted.

(b) It should be noted that in **Section C** questions 1 and 2 each contain a choice.

2 The questions may be answered in any order but all answers are to be written in the spaces provided in this answer book, **and must be written clearly and legibly in ink**.

3 Additional space for answers will be found at the end of the book. If further space is required, supplementary sheets may be obtained from the invigilator and should be inserted inside the **front** cover of this book.

4 The numbers of questions must be clearly inserted with any answers written in the additional space.

5 Rough work, if any should be necessary, should be written in this book and then scored through when the fair copy has been written. If further space is required, a supplementary sheet for rough work may be obtained from the invigilator.

6 Before leaving the examination room you must give this book to the invigilator. If you do not, you may lose all the marks for this paper.

SCOTTISH QUALIFICATIONS AUTHORITY

Read carefully

1. Check that the answer sheet provided is for **Biology Intermediate 2 (Section A)**.
2. For this section of the examination you must use an **HB pencil** and, where necessary, an eraser.
3. Check that the answer sheet you have been given has **your name**, **date of birth**, **SCN** (Scottish Candidate Number) and **Centre Name** printed on it.

   Do not change any of these details.
4. If any of this information is wrong, tell the Invigilator immediately.
5. If this information is correct, **print** your name and seat number in the boxes provided.
6. The answer to each question is **either** A, B, C or D. Decide what your answer is, then, using your pencil, put a horizontal line in the space provided (see sample question below).
7. There is **only one correct** answer to each question.
8. Any rough working should be done on the question paper or the rough working sheet, **not** on your answer sheet.
9. At the end of the exam, put the **answer sheet for Section A inside the front cover of this answer book**.

Sample Question

Plants compete mainly for

A water, light and soil nutrients

B water, food and soil nutrients

C light, water and food

D light, food and soil nutrients.

The correct answer is **A**—water, light and soil nutrients. The answer **A** has been clearly marked in **pencil** with a horizontal line (see below).

Changing an answer

If you decide to change your answer, carefully erase your first answer and using your pencil, fill in the answer you want. The answer below has been changed to **D**.

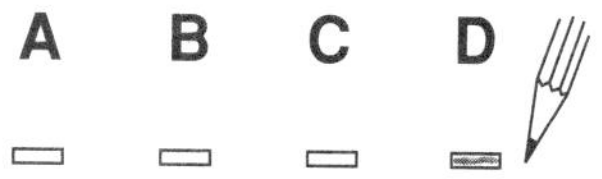

SECTION A

All questions in this Section should be attempted.

1. Which structural feature is common to both plant and animal cells?

A Cell wall

B Chloroplast

C Nucleus

D Large central vacuole

2. Which line in the table below correctly matches the plant cell structure to its function?

	Plant cell structure	*Function*
A	Cytoplasm	Controls all the chemical activities
B	Cell wall	Keeps the cells turgid
C	Vacuole	Prevents the cell from bursting in a hypotonic solution
D	Cell membrane	Controls which molecules enter or leave the cell

3. Once yoghurt has been produced it is stored in a fridge.

This is because

A bacterial growth is slowed down

B it makes the yoghurt more creamy

C it causes lactose to change to lactic acid

D the taste of the yoghurt is improved.

4. The diagram below shows the results of an investigation into the effect of different antibiotics on a type of bacterium.

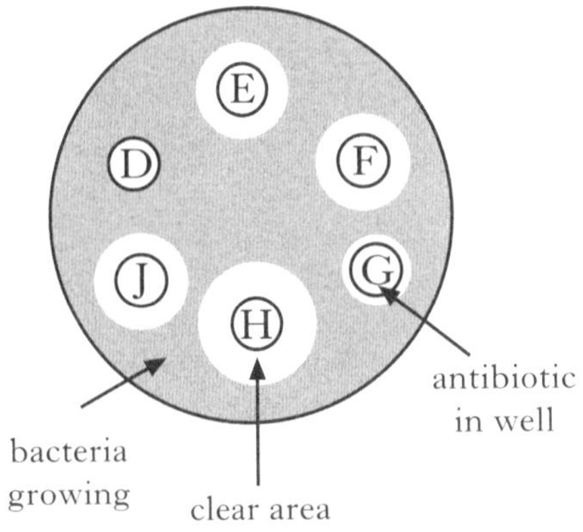

Which of the following conclusions can be drawn from these results?

A These bacteria are resistant to antibiotic H.

B Antibiotic D is the most effective antibiotic against this type of bacterium.

C These bacteria are resistant to antibiotic D.

D This type of bacterium is resistant to all of the antibiotics.

5. The animals present in a sample of leaf litter were counted.

Animals	*Number in sample*
ground beetles	10
woodlice	35
slugs	5
centipedes	10
others	10

What is the percentage of woodlice in the sample?

A 35%

B 50%

C 65%

D 70%

[Turn over

6. The diagram below shows energy transfer within a cell.

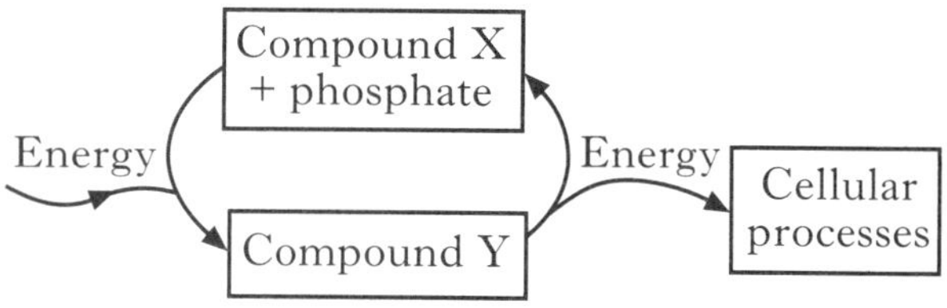

Which line of the table below identifies correctly compounds X and Y?

	X	*Y*
A	glucose	ATP
B	glucose	ADP
C	ADP	ATP
D	ATP	glucose

7. After running a race an athlete experienced muscle fatigue.

Which of the following had increased in the muscles?

A Glucose

B Oxygen

C ATP

D Lactic acid

8. Fermentation of sugar cane produces alcohol. What is produced when this alcohol is mixed with petrol?

A Biogas

B Gasohol

C Methane

D Carbon dioxide

9. Four cylinders of potato tissue were weighed and each was placed into a salt solution of different concentration.

The cylinders were reweighed after one hour. The results are shown in the following table.

	Mass of potato cylinder (g)	
Salt solution	*Initial mass*	*Final mass*
A	10·0	12·6
B	10·0	11·2
C	10·0	9·4
D	10·0	7·0

In which salt solution would most potato cells be plasmolysed?

10. An experiment was carried out to investigate the growth of pea plants kept in a high light intensity following germination.

The graph shows the average shoot length of the pea plants.

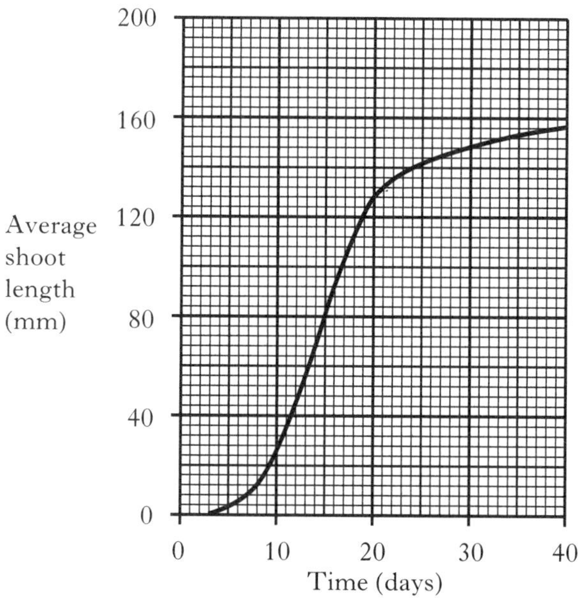

During which 5 day period is there the greatest increase in average shoot length?

A Day 10 – 15

B Day 15 – 20

C Day 20 – 25

D Day 25 – 30

11. The diagram below shows part of a food web in an oak woodland.

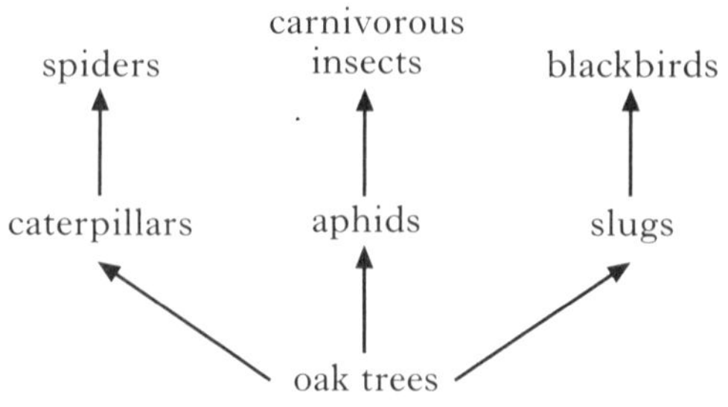

The use of insecticides in a nearby field resulted in the deaths of most aphids and caterpillars.

Which line in the table identifies correctly the effects on the numbers of slugs and carnivorous insects?

	Number of slugs	*Number of carnivorous insects*
A	increases	decreases
B	decreases	stays the same
C	decreases	increases
D	increases	stays the same

12. The diagram below shows a pyramid of biomass.

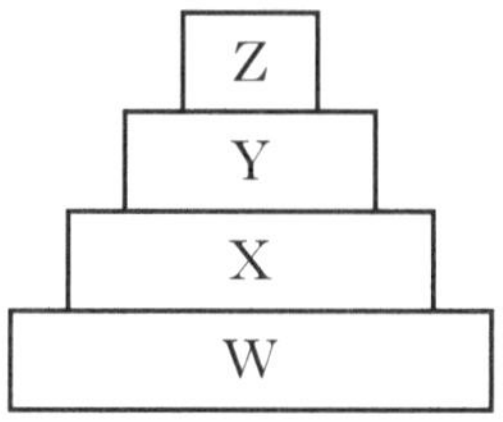

X represents the total mass of

A producers

B primary consumers

C predators

D secondary consumers.

13. Which of the following describes correctly a niche?

A The place where an organism lives

B Organisms and their environments

C A population of organisms in an ecosystem

D The role of an organism in an ecosystem

14. The table below shows the relationship between planting density and the mass of seed harvested for a cereal crop trial.

Planting density (number of plants per square metre)	*Mass of seed harvested* (grams per square metre)
4	60
8	86
15	105
32	77
128	21

What is the percentage increase in mass of seed harvested as planting density increases from 4 to 15 plants per square metre?

A 45%

B 75%

C 90%

D 105%

15. In humans, which of the following gametes are **not** normally formed?

A An egg with an X chromosome

B An egg with a Y chromosome

C A sperm with an X chromosome

D A sperm with a Y chromosome

16. The diagram below shows the same sections of matching chromosomes found in four fruit flies, A, B, C and D.

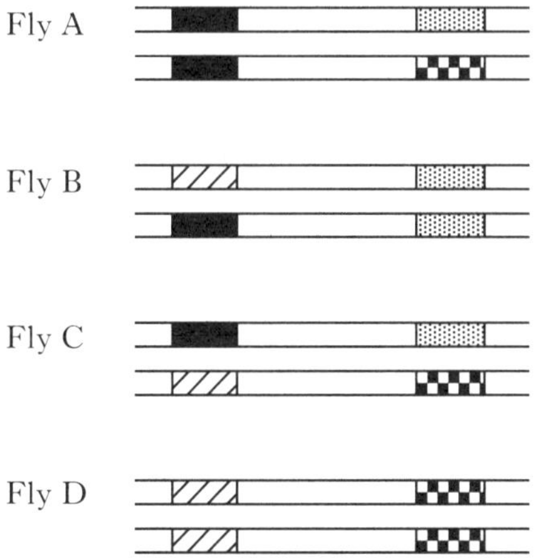

The genes shown on the chromosomes can be identified using the following key.

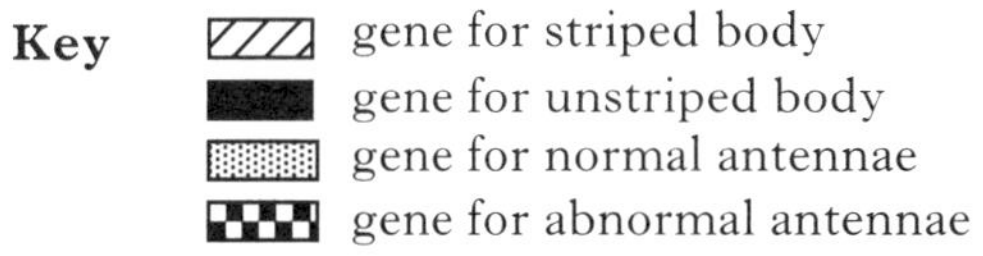

Which fly is homozygous for both genes?

17. The diagram below shows a single villus from the small intestine.

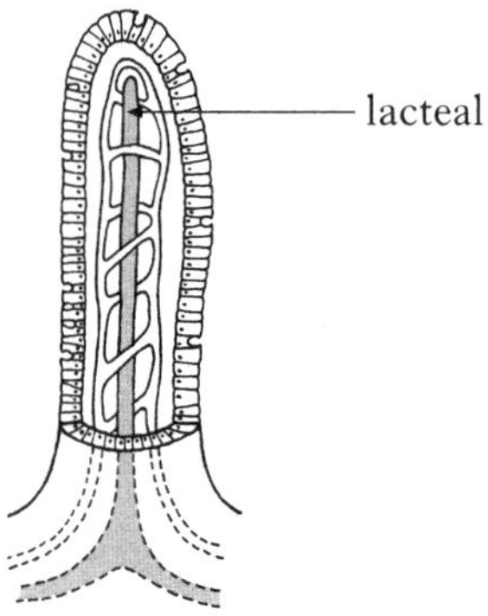

Which food molecules are absorbed into the lacteal?

A Amino acids and glycerol

B Glucose and amino acids

C Fatty acids and glycerol

D Amino acids and fatty acids

18. Which line in the table below describes correctly the changes in food due to digestion?

	Changes in food	
	Molecule size	*Solubility*
A	decreases	increases
B	decreases	decreases
C	increases	decreases
D	increases	increases

19. The diagram shows the apparatus used to investigate the energy content of fat.

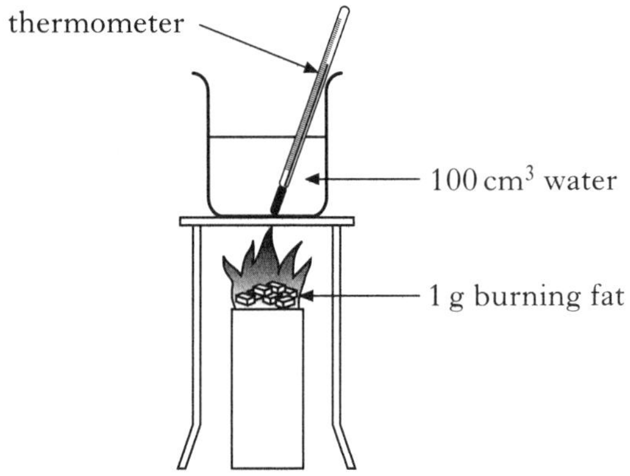

Which of the experiments shown below allows a valid comparison to be made between the energy content of fat and protein?

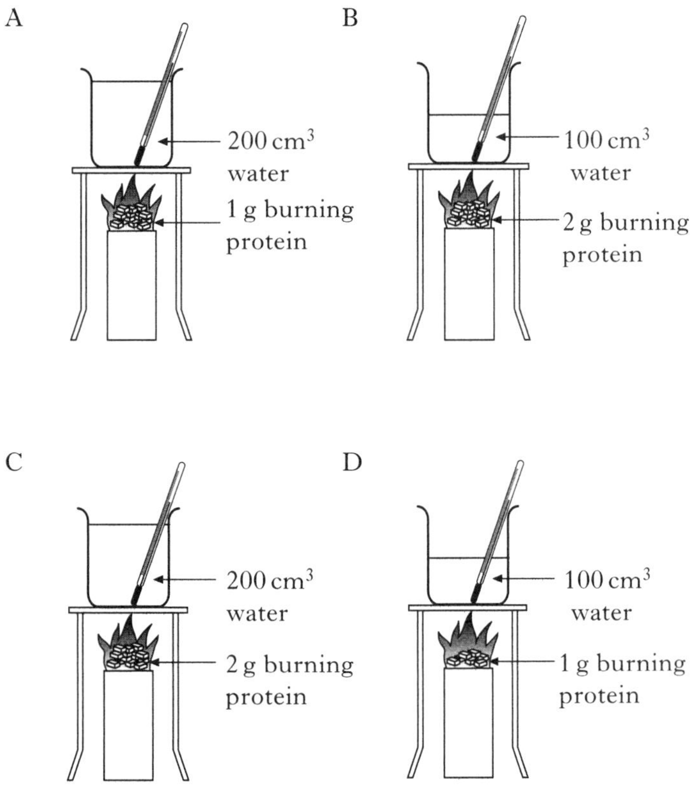

20. Bile is produced in the

A liver

B gall bladder

C stomach

D small intestine.

21. 100 g of baked beans contains 4·5 g of protein.

How many grams of beans would provide a daily protein requirement of 81 g?

A 5·5 g

B 18 g

C 364·5 g

D 1800 g

22. One way that marine bony fish cope with dehydration is

A producing dilute urine

B drinking seawater

C producing large volumes of urine

D absorbing salts.

23. The table below shows some features of blood vessels.

Which line describes features of veins?

	Direction of blood flow	*Detection of pulse*	*Presence of valves*
A	towards the heart	yes	no
B	away from the heart	no	yes
C	towards the heart	no	yes
D	away from the heart	yes	no

24. Which line in the table below identifies correctly how lymphocytes destroy bacteria?

	Phagocytosis	*Antibody production*
A	yes	yes
B	yes	no
C	no	yes
D	no	no

25. The graph below shows the relationship between the concentration of carbon dioxide and oxyhaemoglobin in the blood.

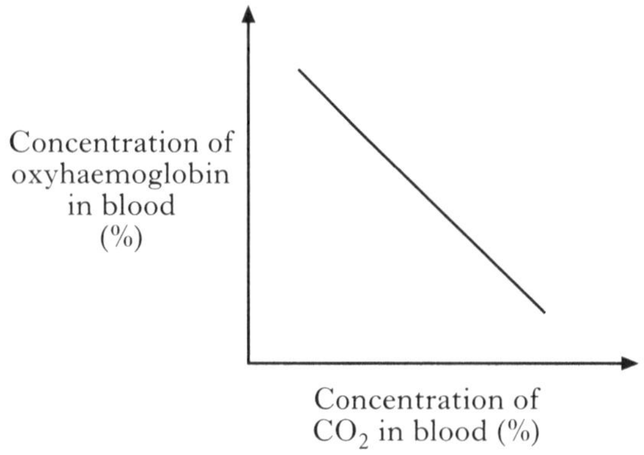

Which of the following describes this relationship?

A As the carbon dioxide concentration decreases, the concentration of oxyhaemoglobin decreases.

B As the carbon dioxide concentration increases, the concentration of oxyhaemoglobin decreases.

C As the carbon dioxide concentration increases, the concentration of oxyhaemoglobin increases.

D As the carbon dioxide concentration increases, it has no effect upon the concentration of oxyhaemoglobin.

Candidates are reminded that the answer sheet for Section A MUST be placed INSIDE the front cover of this answer book.

[Turn over

DO NOT WRITE IN THIS MARGIN

SECTION B

All questions in this section should be attempted.
All answers must be written clearly and legibly in ink.

Marks

1. (*a*) The sentences below describe how oxygen enters the bloodstream for use in respiration.

Underline one option in each set of brackets to make the sentences correct.

Air entering the lungs passes down the {bronchioles / trachea} to the bronchi. 1

To collect oxygen, blood enters the lungs through the pulmonary {artery / vein}

and returns to the {left / right} atrium of the heart. 1

(*b*) The diagram below shows an alveolus in the lungs.

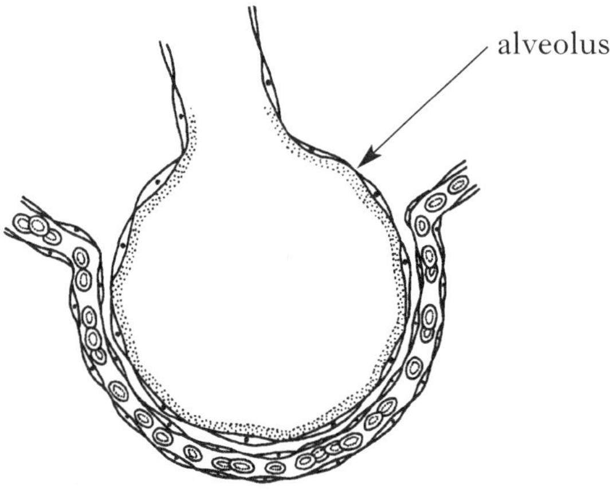

State **two** features of the alveolus that allow efficient gas exchange.

Feature 1 ______________________________ 1

Feature 2 ______________________________ 1

DO NOT WRITE IN THIS MARGIN

Marks

1. (continued)

(*c*) (i) Oxygen diffuses into muscle cells for respiration. Name **one** other raw material needed for respiration that enters by diffusion.

________________________ **1**

(ii) Name a waste product of respiration that diffuses out of muscle cells.

________________________ **1**

(*d*) Osmosis occurs in plant cells.

(i) Name the substance that enters or leaves cells by osmosis.

________________________ **1**

(ii) What term describes the condition of plant cells after being placed in distilled water?

________________________ **1**

[Turn over

DO NOT WRITE IN THIS MARGIN

Marks

2. (*a*) The experiment shown below was set up to demonstrate aerobic respiration in peas that are germinating (starting to grow).

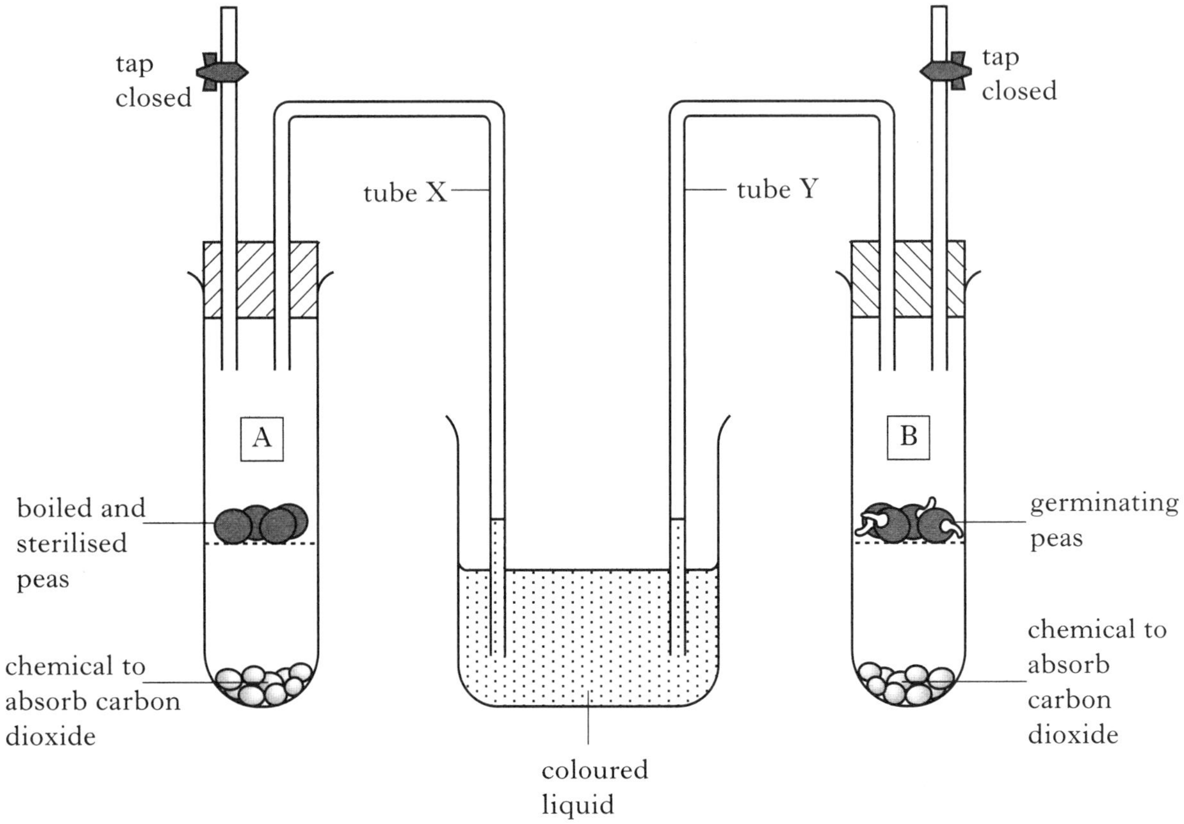

After two days, the level of liquid had risen in tube Y but had not risen in tube X.

(i) Explain the purpose of A as a control in this experiment.

____

____ **1**

(ii) Predict the effect on the level of the liquid in tube Y if a greater mass of peas is used.

____ **1**

DO NOT WRITE IN THIS MARGIN

Marks

2. (continued)

(*b*) The following list contains some features of aerobic and anaerobic respiration in germinating peas.

List

W Does not use oxygen
X Produces carbon dioxide
Y Yields 38 molecules of ATP per glucose molecule
Z Produces ethanol

Complete the table below by writing the letters from the list in the correct columns.

Each letter may be used once or more than once.

Aerobic respiration in germinating peas	*Anaerobic respiration in germinating peas*

2

[Turn over

DO NOT WRITE IN THIS MARGIN

Marks

3. (*a*) A food sample was tested to find which food groups were present.

Both the Benedict's test and the Biuret test were positive.

(i) What colour indicates a positive result with the Benedict's test?

______________________________ **1**

(ii) Which food group was indicated by the Biuret test result?

______________________________ **1**

(*b*) Complete boxes 1 and 2 in the following diagram which shows information about the structures of three food groups.

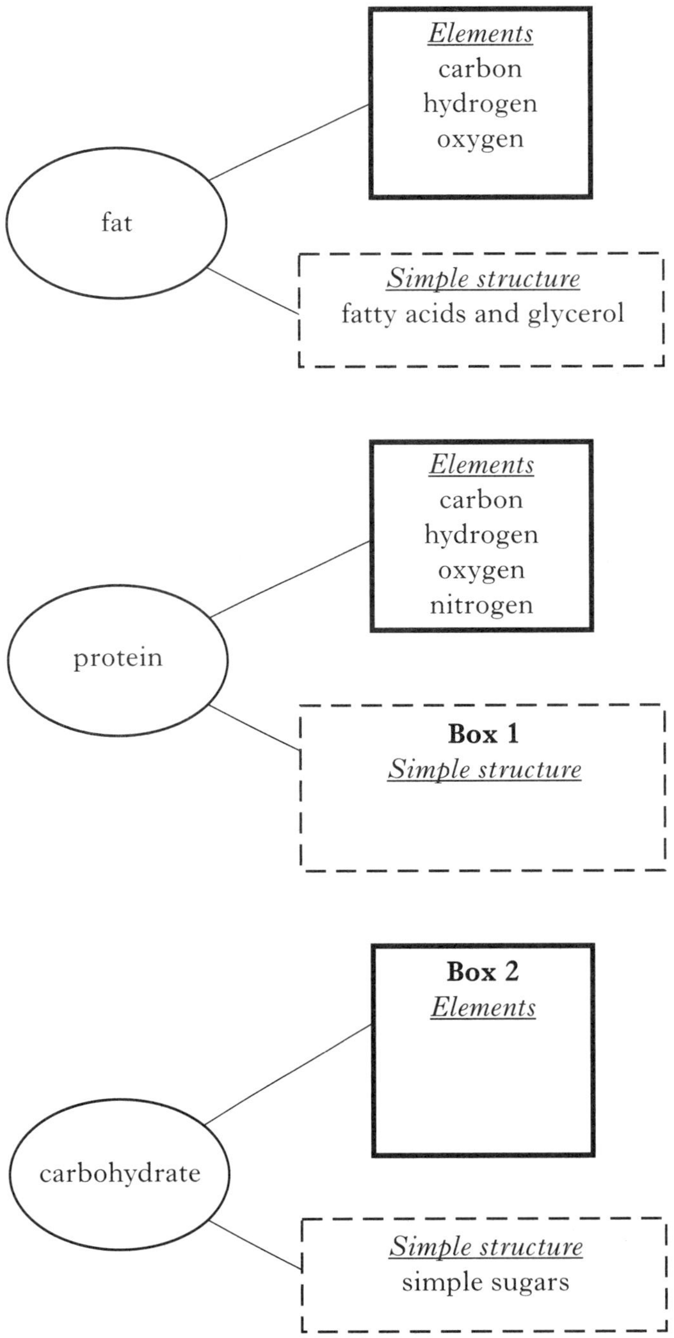

2

DO NOT WRITE IN THIS MARGIN

Marks

3. (continued)

(*c*) The graph below shows the results of an experiment into the activity of a stomach enzyme at various pH levels.

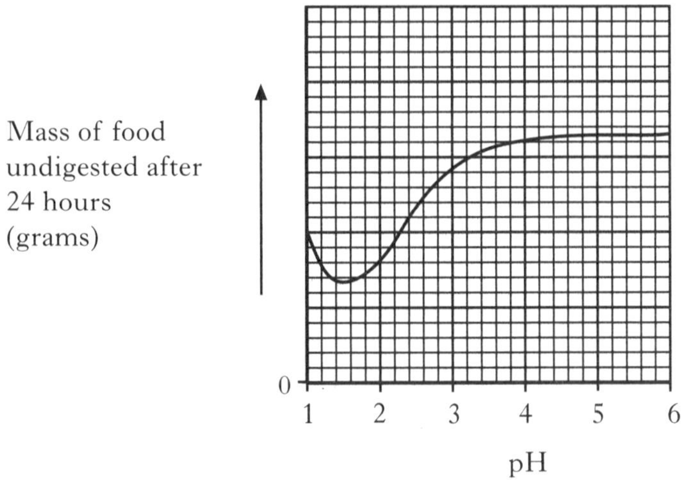

(i) Name a stomach enzyme.

____________________________ **1**

(ii) From the graph, what is the optimum pH of this enzyme?

pH __________ **1**

[Turn over

Marks

4. (*a*) Four groups of students investigated the catalase concentration of different tissues.

Each group set up a test-tube containing 5 cm^3 of hydrogen peroxide and a cube of potato. The oxygen was collected over a 3 minute period and the volume was measured as shown in the diagram below.

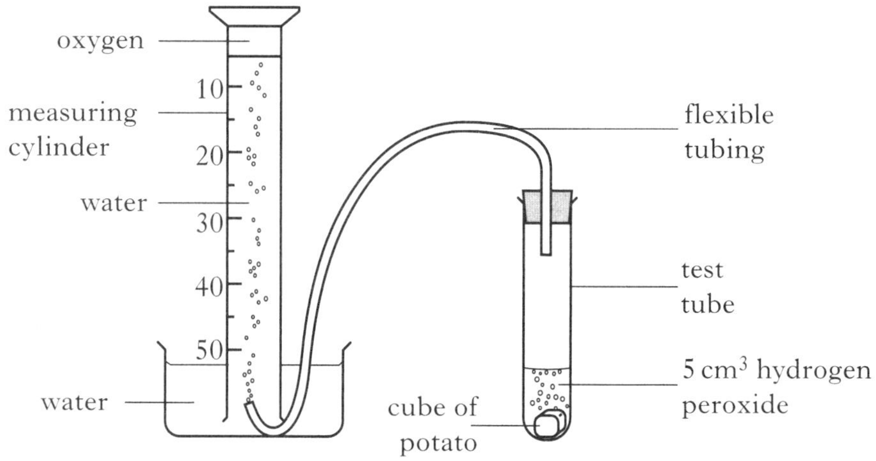

This procedure was repeated by each group using cubes of liver, apple and carrot.

The results from the four groups are given in the table below.

Tissue	*Volume of oxygen collected in 3 minutes* (cm^3)				
	Group 1	*Group 2*	*Group 3*	*Group 4*	*Average*
Potato	5·5	5·0	5·5	6·0	
Liver	39·5	37·0	42·5	35·5	38·5
Apple	1·0	1·5	1·0	0·5	1·0
Carrot	3·5	3·0	3·5	2·0	3·0

(i) Complete the table to show the average volume of oxygen collected for potato tissue.

Space for calculation

1

(ii) The volume of hydrogen peroxide and time taken to collect the oxygen were kept constant in this investigation.

State **two** other variables that must be kept constant.

1 ______________________________ **1**

2 ______________________________ **1**

DO NOT WRITE IN THIS MARGIN

Marks

4. (*a*) (continued)

(iii) What was done in this investigation to make the results reliable?

____

____ **1**

(iv) What conclusion can be drawn from these results?

____

____ **1**

(*b*) The diagram below shows the action of the enzyme phosphorylase in a potato cell.

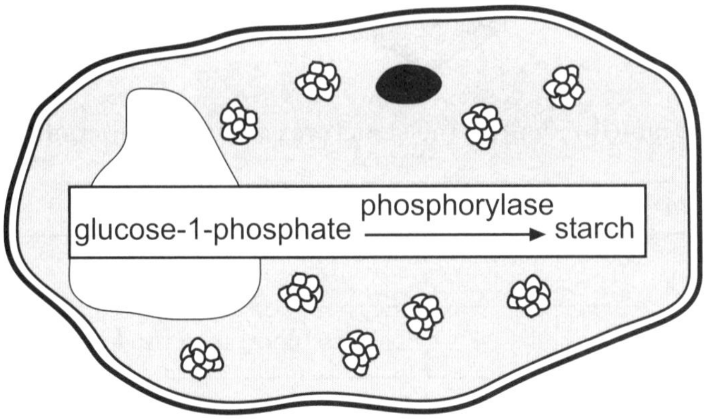

(i) Underline the option in the bracket to make the sentence correct.

The action of the enzyme phosphorylase catalyses the {synthesis / degradation} of starch. **1**

(ii) State the effect of phosphorylase on the rate of this reaction.

____ **1**

(iii) Explain why lipase could not produce starch in this reaction.

____

____ **1**

[Turn over

DO NOT WRITE IN THIS MARGIN

Marks

5. (*a*) The diagram below shows the structure of the human urinary system.

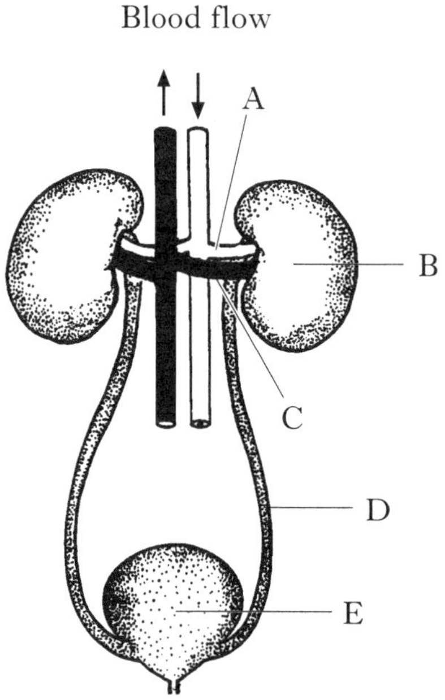

Complete the table to identify the structures and their functions.

Structure	*Letter*	*Function*
Bladder	E	
	A	Carries blood into the kidney
Ureter		Carries urine away from the kidney

2

(*b*) The diagram below represents filtration and reabsorption in the kidney.

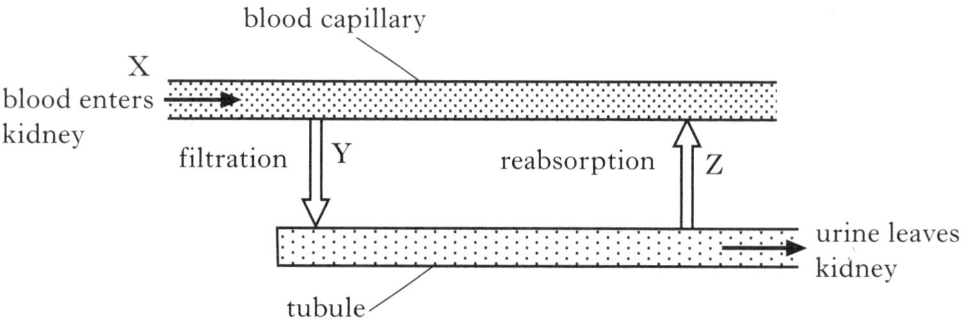

A hormone controls the volume of water reabsorbed at Z.

(i) Name this hormone.

_______________________ 1

(ii) If there is a decrease in the level of this hormone, what will happen to the volume of water reabsorbed at Z?

_______________________ 1

DO NOT WRITE IN THIS MARGIN

Marks

5. (*b*) (continued)

(iii) Tick (✓) the boxes in the table below to indicate which two blood components are filtered out of the blood at Y.

Blood components	*Filtered out at Y*
glucose	
salts	
blood cells	

1

(iv) The rate of flow at X, Y and Z is measured.

Rates of flow:

$X = 1200\,cm^3$ per minute

$Y = 125\,cm^3$ per minute

$Z = 124\,cm^3$ per minute

How much urine will be produced in one hour?

Space for calculation

Volume of urine produced in one hour ____________ cm^3 **1**

[Turn over

DO NOT WRITE IN THIS MARGIN

Marks

6. The three types of neurone involved in the reflex arc for blinking are shown in the diagram below.

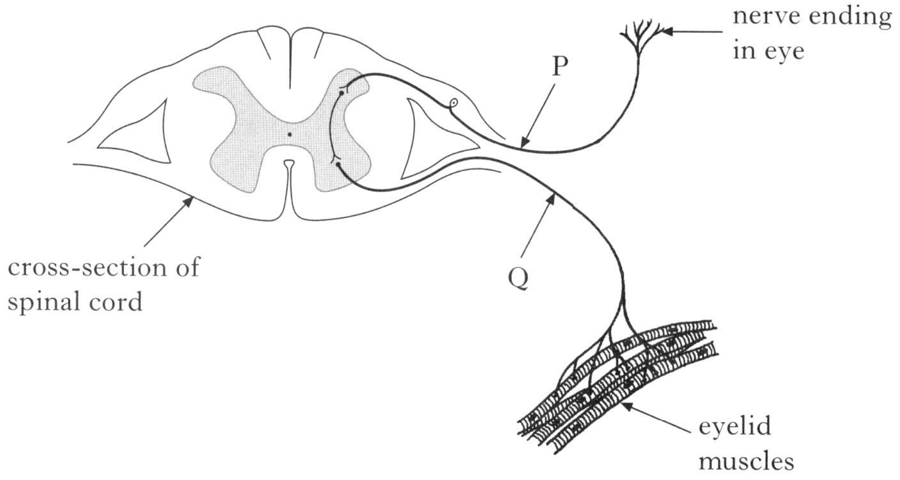

(*a*) Name neurones P and Q.

P ______________________

Q ______________________ **2**

(*b*) Which labelled structure is the effector in this response?

______________________ **1**

(*c*) What is the function of a reflex action?

____

____ **1**

[Turn over for Question 7 on *Page twenty*

DO NOT WRITE IN THIS MARGIN

Marks

7. (*a*) An experiment was set up to measure the effect of light intensity on the rate of photosynthesis in the water plant, *Elodea*.

The light intensity was varied using a dimmer switch on the bulb.

The rate of photosynthesis was measured by counting the number of bubbles released per minute.

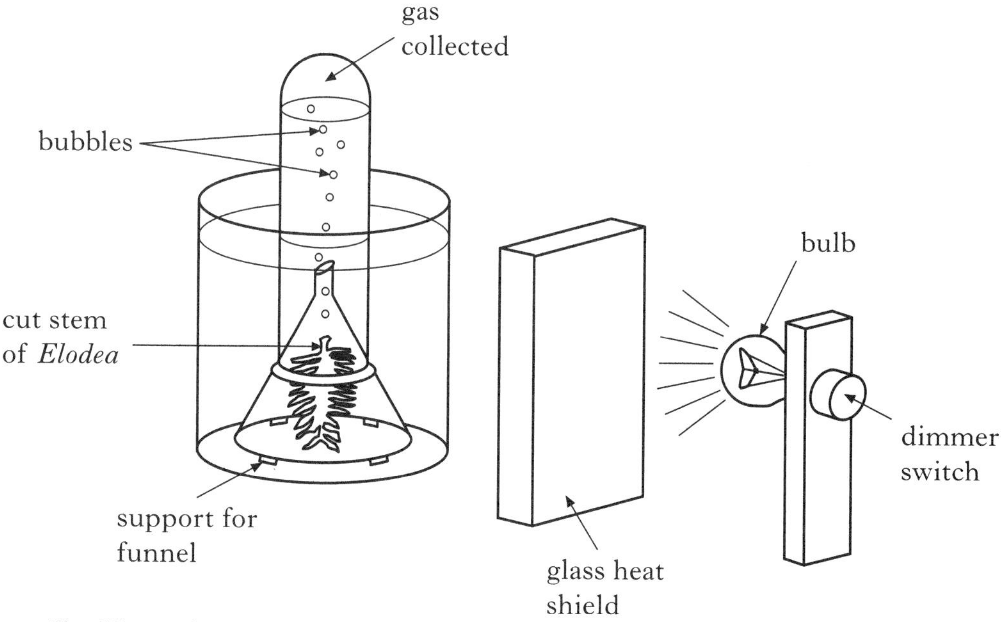

(i) Name the gas collected.

______________________________ **1**

(ii) The results of the experiment are shown in the table below.

Light intensity (units)	*Rate of photosynthesis* (number of bubbles per minute)
1	2
3	10
5	23
8	45
10	45
12	45

DO NOT WRITE IN THIS MARGIN

Marks

7. (*a*) (ii) (continued)

(A) On the grid below, plot a line graph to show rate of photosynthesis against light intensity.

(Additional graph paper, if required, will be found on page 32.)

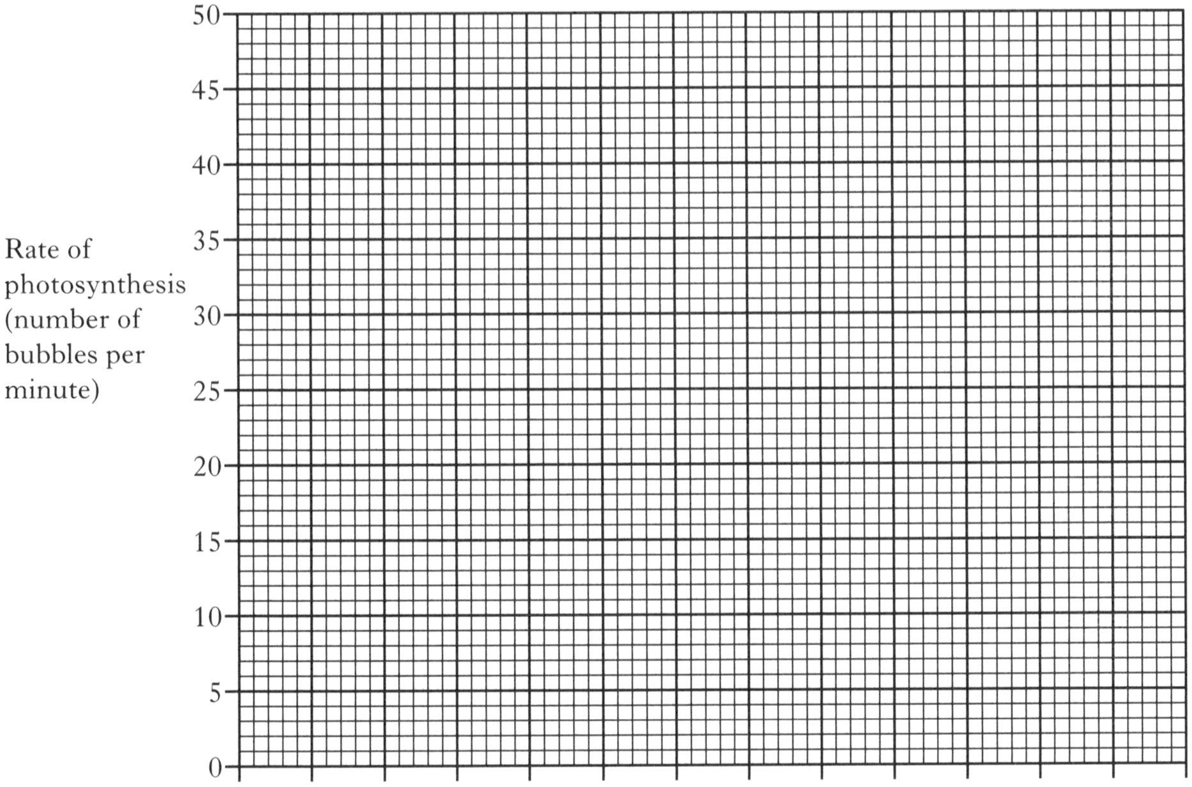

2

(B) Using the data in the table, explain the results obtained at light intensities greater than 8 units.

____

____ 1

(*b*) There are **two** reactions in photosynthesis. The first reaction is photolysis.

(i) Name the two substances produced by photolysis that are required for the second reaction.

Substance 1 ______________________

Substance 2 ______________________ 2

(ii) Name the second reaction.

______________________________ 1

DO NOT WRITE IN THIS MARGIN

Marks

7. (continued)

(*c*) Plant cells convert glucose into other carbohydrates.

Complete the table below by naming two of these carbohydrates.

Role of carbohydrate in plant cells	*Name of carbohydrate*
Storage as an insoluble material	
Forms cell walls	

2

DO NOT WRITE IN THIS MARGIN

Marks

8. (*a*) The diagram below shows a yeast cell.

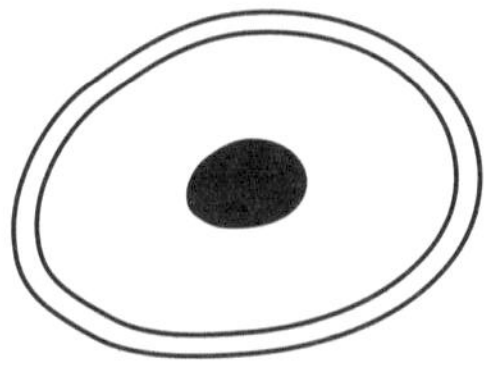

(i) Name the structure shown in the yeast cell which contains the genetic information.

______________________________ **1**

(ii) A molecule consisting of chains of bases is contained in chromosomes.

(A) Name this molecule.

______________________________ **1**

(B) Explain how this molecule controls cell activities.

____

____

______________________________ **2**

(*b*) Gamete production is essential to sexual reproduction.

(i) Name the division of the nucleus that occurs during gamete production.

______________________________ **1**

(ii) Name the process occurring during this division that increases variation.

______________________________ **1**

(iii) Underline **one** option in each set of brackets to make the following sentences correct.

The number of chromosomes in gametes is {half / twice} the number found in body cells.

The zygote is formed by {fusion / division} and contains {half / twice} the number of chromosomes in a gamete. **2**

DO NOT WRITE IN THIS MARGIN

Marks

9. In fowl, the dominant form (R) of one gene determines rose comb shape; single comb shape results from the recessive form (r) of the gene.

The diagram below shows the results of two crosses.

Cross 1 parents	True-breeding rose comb fowl		True-breeding single comb fowl
		↓	
Cross 1 offspring		all rose comb fowl	
Cross 2 parents	Rose comb fowl from Cross 1 offspring	×	Single comb fowl
		↓	
Cross 2 offspring	Rose comb fowl		Single comb fowl
Ratio	1	:	1

(*a*) (i) Which offspring contains only one phenotype?

________________ **1**

(ii) Complete the Punnet square below to show the genotypes of the gametes of the Cross 2 single comb parent and the genotypes of the offspring produced.

<table>
<tr><td colspan="2"></td><td colspan="2">Genotypes of gametes of Cross 2 single comb parent</td></tr>
<tr><td colspan="2"></td><td></td><td></td></tr>
<tr><td rowspan="2">Genotypes of gametes of Cross 2 rose comb parent</td><td>R</td><td></td><td></td></tr>
<tr><td>r</td><td></td><td></td></tr>
</table>

2

DO NOT WRITE IN THIS MARGIN

Marks

9. (continued)

(*b*) Decide if each of the following statements is **True** or **False**, and tick (✓) the appropriate box.

If the statement is **False**, write the correct word in the **Correction** box to replace the word underlined in the statement.

Statement	*True*	*False*	*Correction*
A characteristic controlled by many genes is called co-dominant.			
The gene for comb shape has two different alleles.			
True breeding is another way of describing a homozygous individual.			

3

[Turn over

Marks

10. The small burrowing invertebrate, *Corophium*, is found in the mud of Scottish estuaries.

Corophium (magnified × 6)

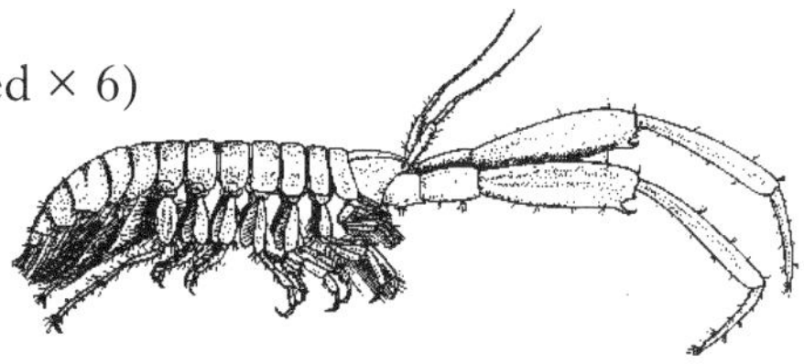

Corophium is the major prey of many species of migratory wading birds. These birds are present in large numbers from August to April.

The graph below shows the results of a one year survey on the numbers of *Corophium* taken on the first day of each month.

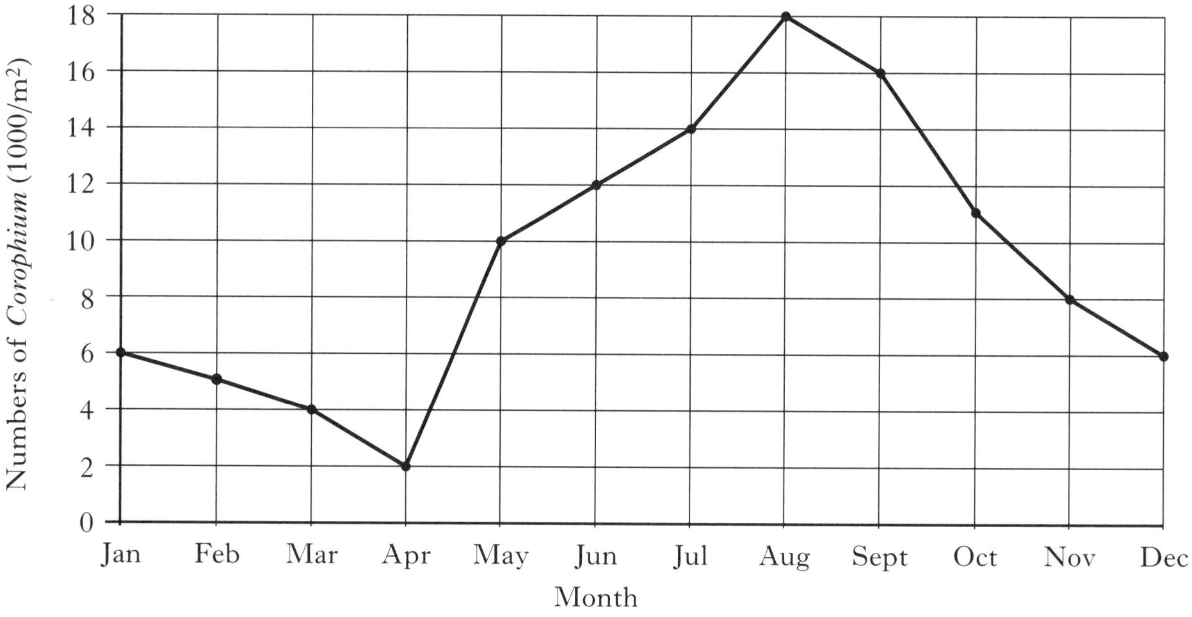

(*a*) Describe the changes in the numbers of *Corophium* from January to December.

____

____

____ **2**

(*b*) How many times greater are the numbers of *Corophium* on 1st June compared to 1st April?

Space for calculation

____________ times **1**

DO NOT WRITE IN THIS MARGIN

Marks

10. (continued)

(*c*) Using all the information given, explain why there are high numbers of *Corophium* on 1st August.

____

____ **1**

(*d*) Predict what would happen to the biodiversity of this estuary if the wading birds stayed all year. Explain your answer.

Prediction ______________________________________ **1**

Explanation ______________________________________

____ **1**

[Turn over for Section C on *page twenty-eight*

DO NOT WRITE IN THIS MARGIN

SECTION C

Marks

Both questions in this section should be attempted.

Note that each question contains a choice.

Questions 1 and 2 should be attempted on the blank pages which follow. All answers must be written clearly and legibly in ink.

Supplementary sheets, if required, may be obtained from the invigilator.

1. Answer **either** A **or** B.

A. The diagram below shows human blood as seen through a microscope.

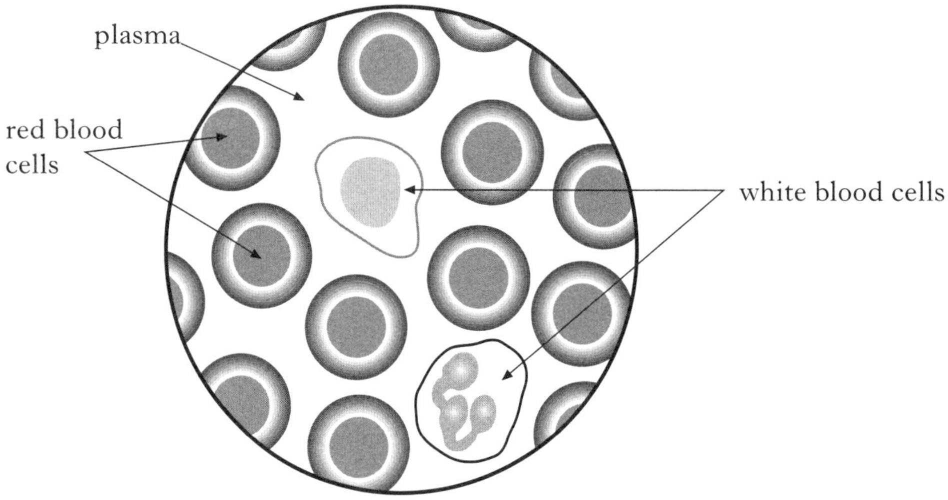

(*a*) Name the **two** parts of the blood involved in the transport of substances around the body.

(*b*) Describe how named substances are transported by each part of the blood. **5**

OR

B. The diagram below shows a section through the brain.

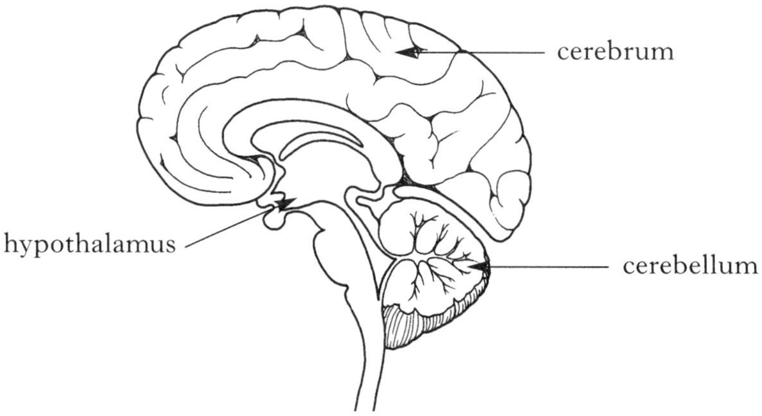

(*a*) Name the part of the brain that regulates body temperature.

(*b*) State its response to a **decrease** in body temperature by describing the changes which will occur in the skin, blood vessels and muscles. **5**

Question 2 is on *Page thirty*.

DO NOT WRITE IN THIS MARGIN

SPACE FOR ANSWER TO QUESTION 1

[Turn over for Question 2 on *Page thirty*

DO NOT WRITE IN THIS MARGIN

Marks

2. Answer **either** A **or** B.

Labelled diagrams may be included where appropriate.

A. Genetic engineering uses bacteria to produce human insulin. Describe the stages involved in this process. **5**

OR

B. Describe the process of natural selection as illustrated by the peppered moth *Biston betularia*. **5**

[*END OF QUESTION PAPER*]

DO NOT WRITE IN THIS MARGIN

SPACE FOR ANSWER TO QUESTION 2

DO NOT WRITE IN THIS MARGIN

ADDITIONAL SPACE FOR ANSWERS

ADDITIONAL GRAPH PAPER FOR QUESTION 7(*a*)(ii)A

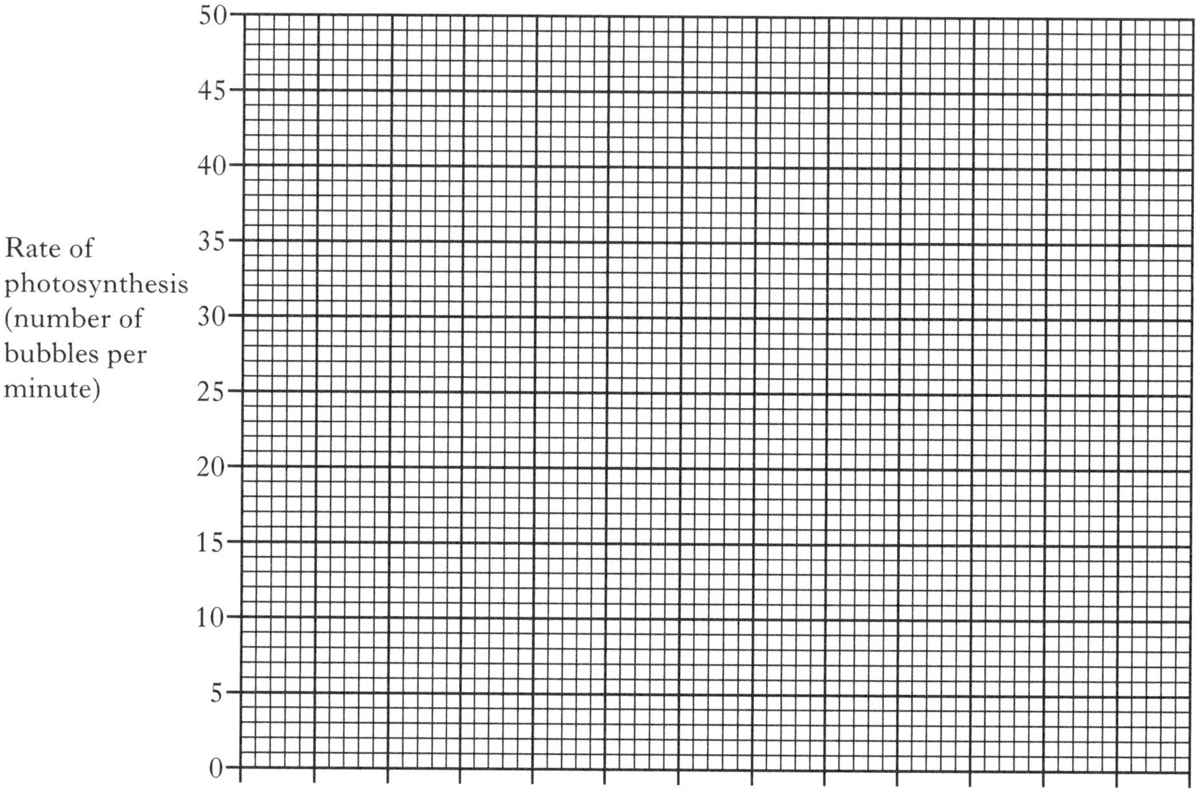

DO NOT WRITE IN THIS MARGIN

ADDITIONAL SPACE FOR ANSWERS

DO NOT WRITE IN THIS MARGIN

ADDITIONAL SPACE FOR ANSWERS

INTERMEDIATE 2

2008

[BLANK PAGE]

FOR OFFICIAL USE

Total for Sections B and C

X007/201

NATIONAL QUALIFICATIONS 2008

TUESDAY, 27 MAY
9.00 AM – 11.00 AM

BIOLOGY
INTERMEDIATE 2

Fill in these boxes and read what is printed below.

Full name of centre

Town

Forename(s)

Surname

Date of birth
Day Month Year

Scottish candidate number

Number of seat

SECTION A (25 marks)

Instructions for completion of Section A are given on page two.

For this section of the examination you must use an HB pencil.

SECTIONS B AND C (75 marks)

1 (a) All questions should be attempted.

(b) It should be noted that in **Section C** questions 1 and 2 each contain a choice.

2 The questions may be answered in any order but all answers are to be written in the spaces provided in this answer book, **and must be written clearly and legibly in ink**.

3 Additional space for answers will be found at the end of the book. If further space is required, supplementary sheets may be obtained from the invigilator and should be inserted inside the **front** cover of this book.

4 The numbers of questions must be clearly inserted with any answers written in the additional space.

5 Rough work, if any should be necessary, should be written in this book and then scored through when the fair copy has been written. If further space is required, a supplementary sheet for rough work may be obtained from the invigilator.

6 Before leaving the examination room you must give this book to the invigilator. If you do not, you may lose all the marks for this paper.

Read carefully

1 Check that the answer sheet provided is for **Biology Intermediate 2 (Section A)**.

2 For this section of the examination you must use an **HB pencil** and, where necessary, an eraser.

3 Check that the answer sheet you have been given has **your name**, **date of birth**, **SCN** (Scottish Candidate Number) and **Centre Name** printed on it.

Do not change any of these details.

4 If any of this information is wrong, tell the Invigilator immediately.

5 If this information is correct, **print** your name and seat number in the boxes provided.

6 The answer to each question is **either** A, B, C or D. Decide what your answer is, then, using your pencil, put a horizontal line in the space provided (see sample question below).

7 There is **only one correct** answer to each question.

8 Any rough working should be done on the question paper or the rough working sheet, **not** on your answer sheet.

9 At the end of the exam, put the **answer sheet for Section A inside the front cover of this answer book**.

Sample Question

Plants compete mainly for

A water, light and soil nutrients

B water, food and soil nutrients

C light, water and food

D light, food and soil nutrients.

The correct answer is **A**—water, light and soil nutrients. The answer **A** has been clearly marked in **pencil** with a horizontal line (see below).

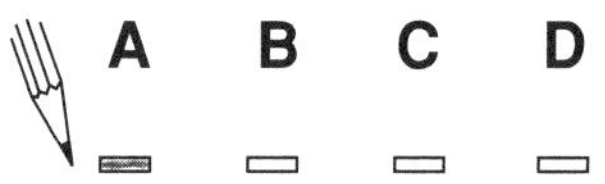

Changing an answer

If you decide to change your answer, carefully erase your first answer and using your pencil, fill in the answer you want. The answer below has been changed to **D**.

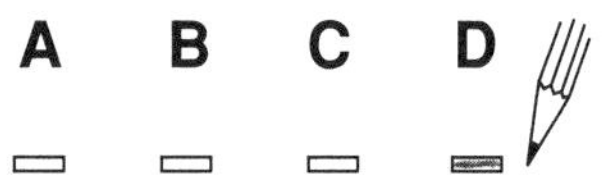

SECTION A

All questions in this Section should be attempted.

1. The diagrams below show four cells.

Which cell is a leaf mesophyll cell?

A

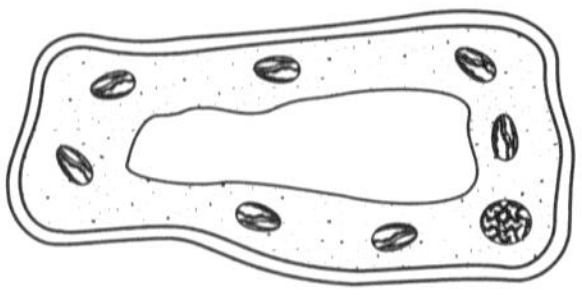

B

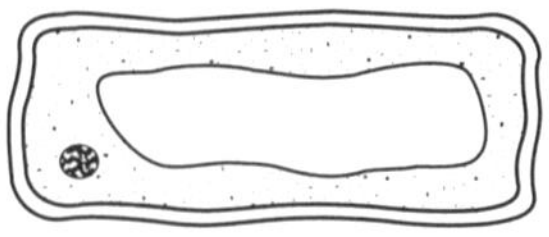

C

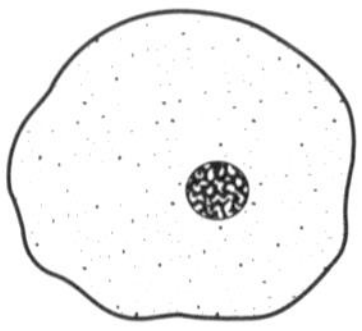

D

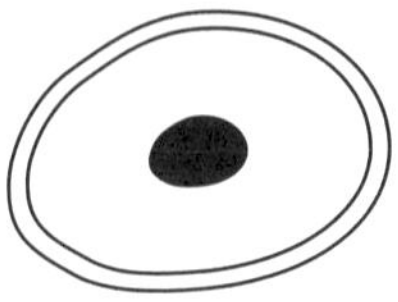

2. Which line in the table below identifies correctly the importance of diffusion to an animal cell?

	Raw material gained	*Waste product removed*
A	oxygen	glucose
B	carbon dioxide	oxygen
C	oxygen	carbon dioxide
D	glucose	oxygen

3. Which of the following molecules can both diffuse through a cell membrane?

A Amino acids and starch

B Amino acids and water

C Starch and protein

D Protein and water

4. Red blood cells burst when they are placed in water because

A the cell contents are hypotonic to the water

B the cell contents are isotonic to the water

C the water is hypotonic to the cell contents

D the water is hypertonic to the cell contents.

5. The energy yield per glucose molecule during aerobic respiration is

A 2 molecules of ATP

B 18 molecules of ATP

C 36 molecules of ATP

D 38 molecules of ATP.

6. The following are statements about respiration.

1 ATP is produced

2 Lactic acid is produced

3 Carbon dioxide is produced

4 Ethanol is produced

Which of the statements are true of anaerobic respiration in human muscle tissue?

A 2 only

B 2 and 3 only

C 1 and 2 only

D 1, 3 and 4 only

7. The role of chlorophyll in photosynthesis is to trap

A light energy for ATP production

B chemical energy for ATP production

C light energy for ADP production

D chemical energy for ADP production.

8. The raw materials for photosynthesis are

A carbon dioxide and water

B oxygen and water

C carbon dioxide and glucose

D oxygen and glucose.

9. All proteins are composed of

A genes

B DNA

C amino acids

D bases.

10. Which of the following diagrams best represents the arrangement of chromosomes in a cell undergoing meiosis?

A

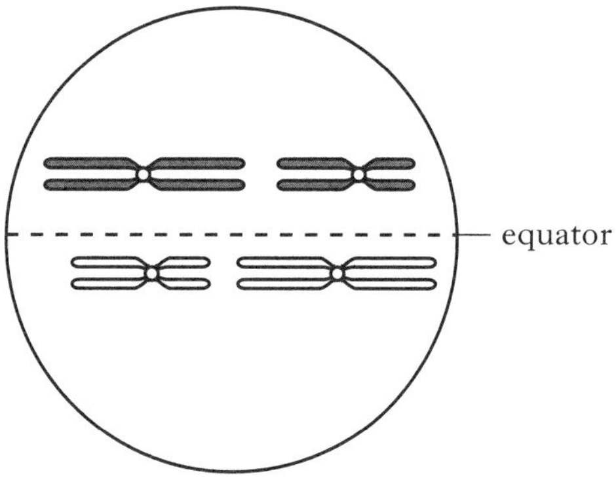

B

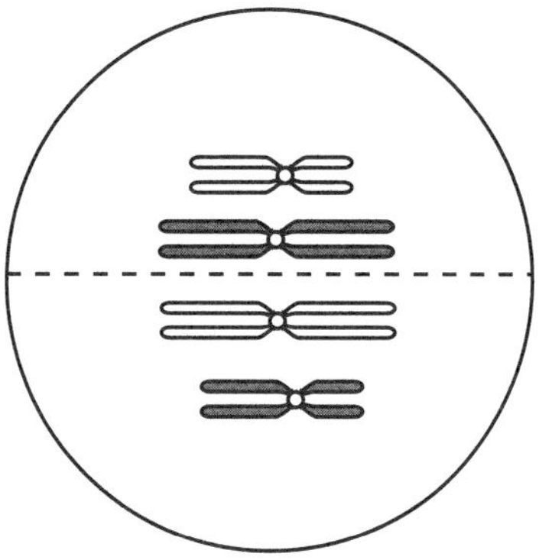

C

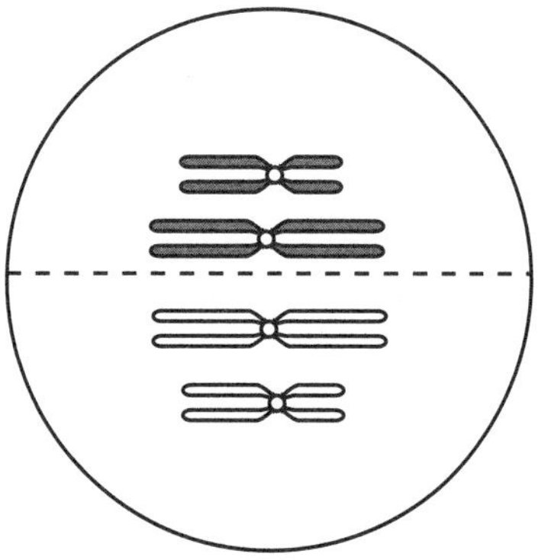

D

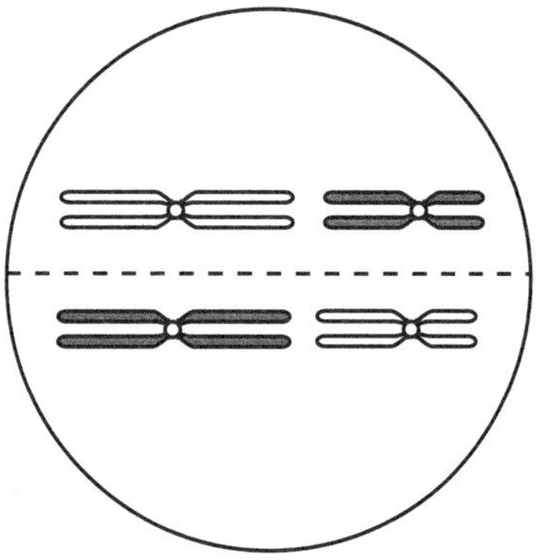

11. Which line in the table describes correctly the possible chromosome content of human gametes?

	Sperm		*Ovum (egg)*	
	Total number of chromosomes	*Type of sex chromosome*	*Total number of chromosomes*	*Type of sex chromosome*
A	23	X	23	Y
B	23	Y	23	X
C	46	X	46	Y
D	46	Y	46	X

12. In the fruit fly *Drosophila*, the allele for normal wings is dominant to the allele for short wings.

A normal winged fly was crossed with a short winged fly and all the F_1 offspring had normal wings.

If these F_1 offspring were to mate with each other, what percentage of the F_2 offspring would be expected to have normal wings?

A 25%

B 50%

C 75%

D 100%

13. The diagram below shows the same sections of matching chromosomes found in four fruit flies, A, B, C and D.

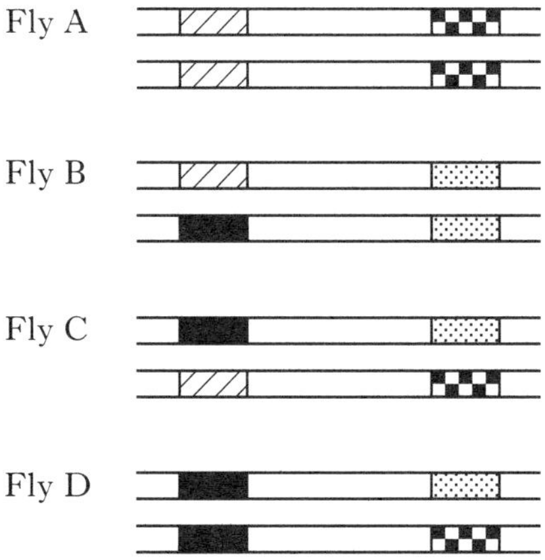

The genes shown on the chromosomes can be identified using the following key.

Key

dominant gene for striped body
recessive gene for unstriped body
dominant gene for normal antennae
recessive gene for abnormal antennae

Which fly has a striped body and abnormal antennae?

14. In a breed of dog, the alleles for white coat colour and black coat colour are **co-dominant**.

A cross was performed between two heterozygous dogs.

Which line in the table below shows the numbers of different phenotypes and genotypes which are possible in the offspring?

	Number of phenotypes	*Number of genotypes*
A	1	3
B	2	3
C	3	2
D	3	3

15. Which of the following is an example of natural selection?

A Increased milk yield in dairy cattle

B Industrial melanism in Peppered Moths

C Insulin production by bacteria

D Insertion of DNA into a chromosome

16. The Peppered Moth is found in two distinct forms. One form is dark coloured and the other is light coloured. The moths rest on the trunks of trees.

Pale coloured tree-trunks in an area were darkened by pollution. What would happen to the numbers of the two forms of the Peppered Moth in that area?

A The numbers of each form would increase.

B The dark form would increase and the light form decrease.

C The numbers of each form would decrease.

D The light form would increase and the dark form decrease.

17. Which of the following is **not** a benefit of selective breeding in crop plants?

A Higher yields can be produced.

B Undesirable features can be eliminated.

C Seed quality can be improved.

D Higher yields can always be guaranteed.

18. Lipase is an enzyme found in the small intestine. Lipase speeds up the breakdown of fat. Full cream milk contains a high proportion of fat.

Three test tubes were set up as shown in the diagram below.

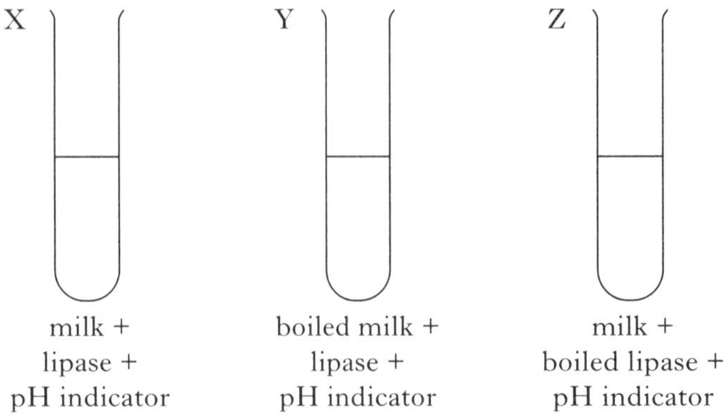

The pH of the contents of each test tube was recorded at the start and again 15 minutes later.

What changes in pH took place?

A The pH decreased in each test tube.

B The pH increased in each test tube.

C The pH decreased in tubes X and Y and did not change in tube Z.

D The pH increased in tubes Y and Z and did not change in tube X.

[Turn over

19. The diagram below shows the apparatus used to investigate the energy contents of different foods.

1 g of each food was burned under a beaker containing 100 cm^3 of water. The rise in water temperature was measured using a thermometer.

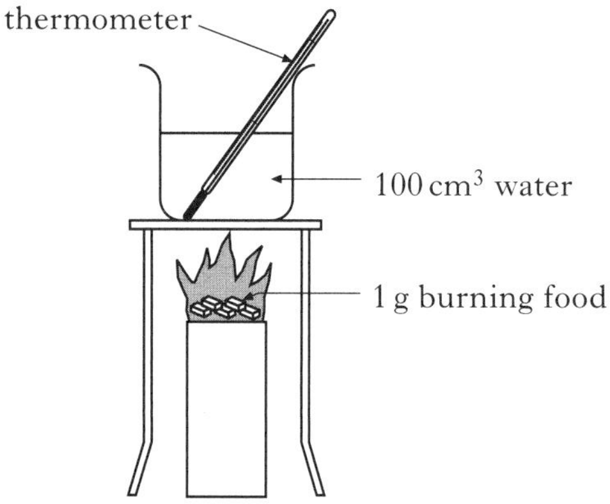

When different foods were burned, the following results were obtained.

Food	*Temperature rise* (°C)
potato	15
margarine	40
egg	20

The following equation can be used to calculate the energy value of food.

Energy value = 0·42 × temperature rise (°C)
(kJ per gram)

Using this equation, the energy value of egg is

A 0·42

B 8·4

C 84

D 840.

20. The energy values of different food groups are shown in the table.

Food group	*Energy value* (kJ per gram)
Carbohydrate	19
Fat	38
Protein	19

What is the simple whole number ratio of the energy value in fat to protein to carbohydrate?

A 1 : 2 : 1

B 2 : 1 : 1

C 19 : 38 : 19

D 38 : 19 : 19

21. The following statements refer to the state of muscles in the gut.

Statement	*State of muscles*
1	contracted in front of food
2	relaxed in front of food
3	contracted behind food
4	relaxed behind food

Which statements describe peristalsis?

A 2 and 3

B 1 and 3

C 1 and 4

D 2 and 4

22. Tests were carried out on a sample of food. The result of each test is shown in the table below.

Food test	*Iodine solution*	*Benedict's solution*	*Biuret solution*	*Translucent spot*
Result	negative	negative	positive	negative

The sample of food contained

A glucose

B protein

C starch

D fat.

23. Carbon dioxide is removed from the body through the lungs. The correct pathway taken by a molecule of carbon dioxide out of the lungs is

A alveoli → bronchioles → bronchi → trachea

B trachea → bronchi → bronchioles → alveoli

C alveoli → bronchi → bronchioles → trachea

D trachea → bronchioles → bronchi → alveoli.

24. The graph shows the percentage saturation of haemoglobin at different oxygen concentrations.

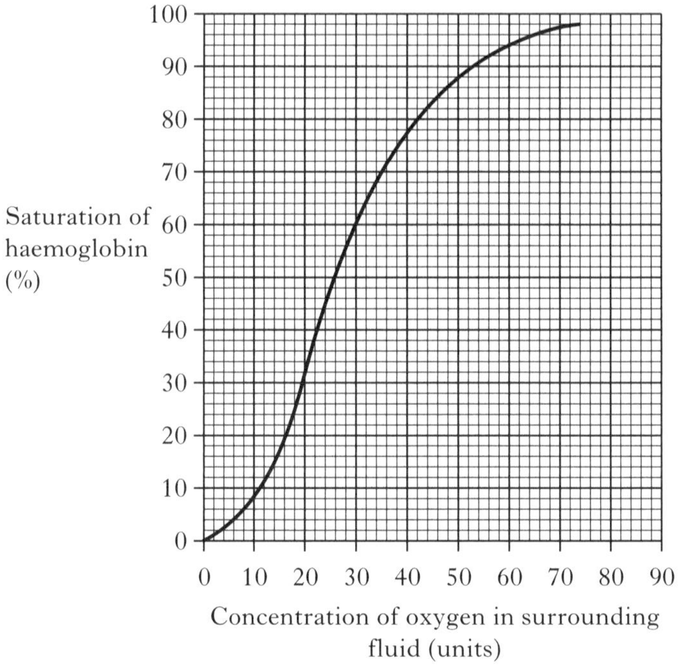

What is the percentage saturation of haemoglobin with oxygen when the oxygen concentration of the surroundings is 60 units?

A 30

B 90

C 92

D 94

25. The diagram below shows a side view of the human brain.

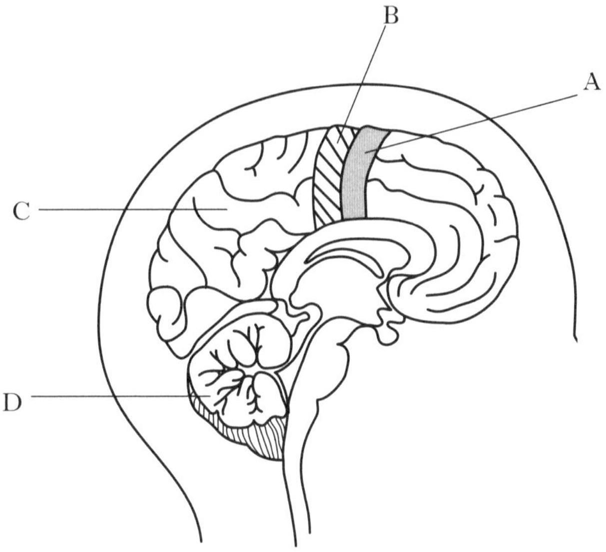

Which label identifies correctly the part of the brain which controls balance?

Candidates are reminded that the answer sheet for Section A MUST be placed INSIDE the front cover of this answer book.

[Turn over

[BLANK PAGE]

DO NOT WRITE IN THIS MARGIN

SECTION B

Marks

All questions in this section should be attempted.
All answers must be written clearly and legibly in ink.

1. (*a*) *Euglena* is a single celled organism.
The diagram below shows some of the structures within *Euglena*.

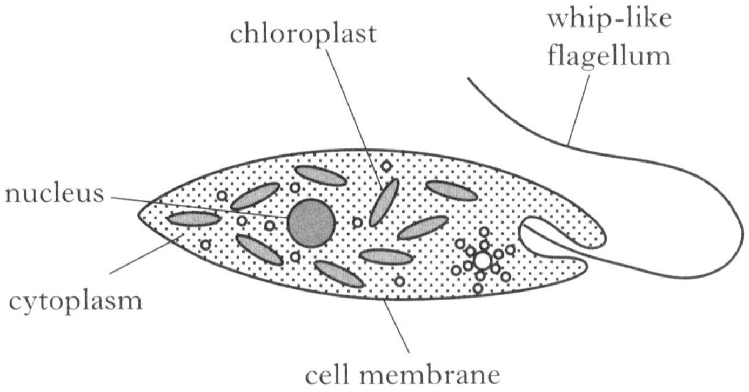

(i) *Euglena* has structures found in most cells.

Complete the table below to show the names of these structures and their functions.

Structure	*Function*
	controls the entry and exit of materials
Cytoplasm	
Nucleus	

2

(ii) Name the structure that identifies *Euglena* as a plant cell.

______________________________ 1

(*b*) Most plant cells have a cell wall.

Name the structural carbohydrate in the cell wall.

______________________________ 1

[Turn over

DO NOT WRITE IN THIS MARGIN

Marks

2. Photosynthesis is the process by which green plants make glucose using energy from the sun.

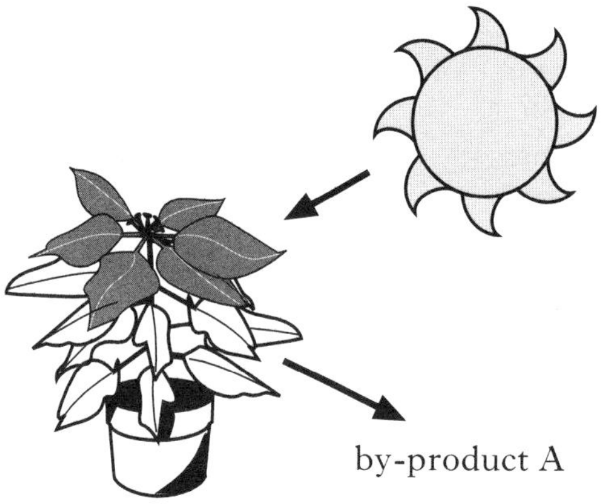

(*a*) Name the by-product A released during photosynthesis.

______________________________ **1**

(*b*) Hydrogen and a high energy molecule are produced during photolysis.

(i) Name the high energy molecule.

______________________________ **1**

(ii) Describe the use of hydrogen in carbon fixation.

______________________________ **1**

(*c*) (i) Explain why an increase in temperature can lead to an increase in the rate of photosynthesis.

____

______________________________ **2**

(ii) Other than temperature, state **two** limiting factors of photosynthesis.

1. ______________________________

2. ______________________________ **1**

DO NOT WRITE IN THIS MARGIN

Marks

3. (*a*) The diagram below shows the link between aerobic respiration and protein synthesis.

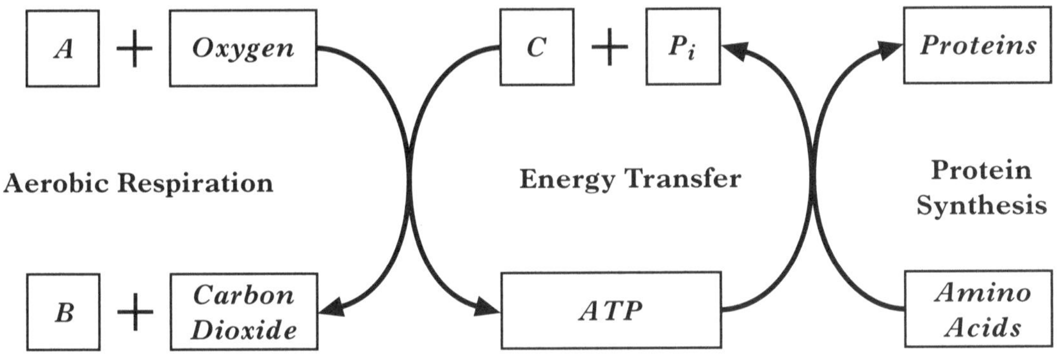

(i) Name substances A, B and C.

A ______________________________

B ______________________________

C ______________________________ **2**

(ii) Some energy released in respiration can be used for protein synthesis.

State one other cellular activity that uses energy.

______________________________ **1**

(*b*) The graph below shows lactic acid concentration in blood during a period of vigorous exercise (P) and of complete rest (Q).

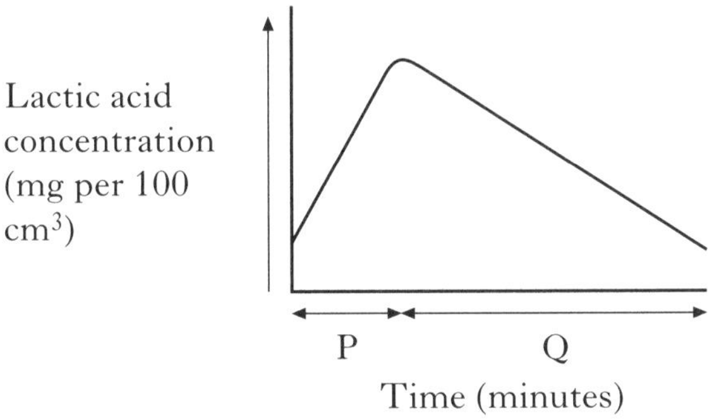

Explain why the lactic acid concentration changes during period Q.

____

____ **1**

[Turn over

DO NOT WRITE IN THIS MARGIN

Marks

4. A student cut five similar cylinders from the same potato, dried them with a paper towel and weighed them.

Each cylinder was placed in a different concentration of sugar solution as shown in the diagram below:

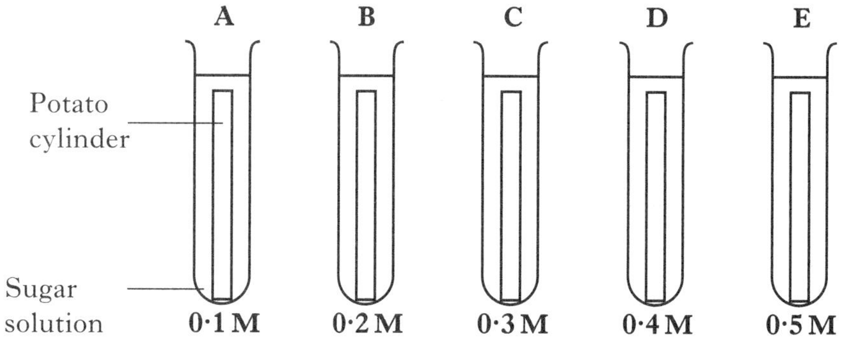

After three hours, the student removed the cylinders from the solutions, dried and weighed them as before.

The results are shown in the table below.

Test tube	*Concentration of sugar solution* (M)	*Initial mass of potato cylinder* (g)	*Final mass of potato cylinder* (g)	*Change in mass of potato cylinder* (g)	*Percentage change in mass of potato*
A	0·1	2·0	2·2	+0·2	+10
B	0·2	2·0	2·1	+0·1	+5
C	0·3	2·0	1·8	–0·2	–10
D	0·4	2·0	1·7	–0·3	
E	0·5	2·0	1·5	–0·5	–25

(*a*) Complete the table by calculating the **percentage change in mass** of the potato cylinder in 0·4 M sugar solution.

Space for calculation

1

(*b*) (i) Name the variable altered in this investigation.

____ **1**

(ii) Suggest one way in which the reliability of the results could be improved.

____ **1**

DO NOT WRITE IN THIS MARGIN

Marks

4. (*b*) (continued)

(iii) Would the results be valid if the cylinders were **not** dried before being weighed? Tick (✓) the correct box.

Valid ☐ Not valid ☐

Explain your answer.

Explanation ______________________________

____

______________________________ **1**

(*c*) (i) State the letter of one test tube containing a potato cylinder in a **hypertonic** solution.

Letter __________ **1**

(ii) Predict the appearance of the potato cylinder in test tube E after three hours.

______________________________ **1**

[Turn over

DO NOT WRITE IN THIS MARGIN

Marks

5. The pictures show some organisms from a marine ecosystem.

The pictures are not to scale.

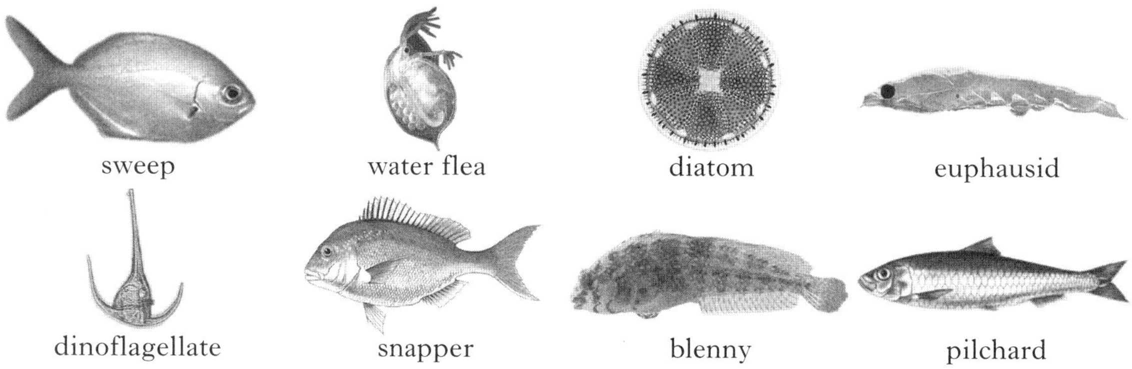

The table below shows information about the feeding relationships in the marine ecosystem.

Organism	*Food eaten*
euphasid	dinoflagellate, diatom
dinoflagellate	none
sweep	diatom
snapper	sweep, pilchard, blenny
pilchard	water flea, euphausid
blenny	water flea, euphausid
diatom	none
water flea	diatom, dinoflagellate

(*a*) (i) Use the information in the table to complete the food web below.

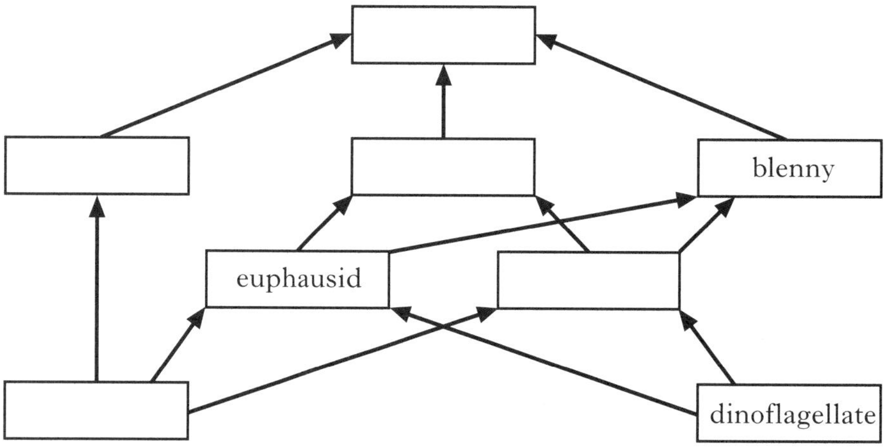

2

(ii) What term is used to describe the snapper in this ecosystem?

______________________________ **1**

DO NOT WRITE IN THIS MARGIN

Marks

5. (continued)

(*b*) A pod of dolphins arrived in the area. Dolphins feed on snappers.

Describe the effect of the dolphins on the size of the euphausid population. Explain your answer.

Effect ______________________________ **1**

Explanation ______________________________

______________________________ **1**

[Turn over

DO NOT WRITE IN THIS MARGIN

Marks

6. The table shows the number of pilot whales caught in the Faroe islands between 1994 and 2000.

Year	*Number of pilot whales caught*
1994	1200
1995	228
1996	1500
1997	1170
1998	820
1999	610
2000	580

(*a*) (i) Construct a **bar graph** of the results given from **1996** to **2000**.

(Additional graph paper, if required, will be found on page 32)

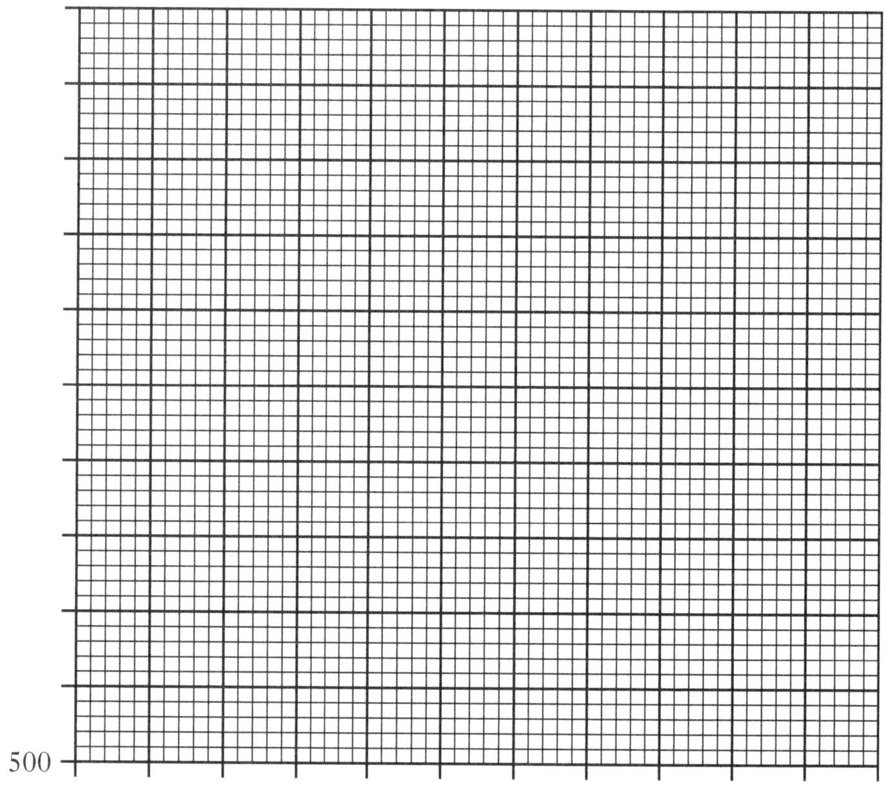

3

DO NOT WRITE IN THIS MARGIN

Marks

6. (*a*) (continued)

(ii) Describe the trend shown by the results in the table from **1996** to **2000**.

____

____ **1**

(iii) What is the average yearly pilot whale catch from **1996** to **2000**?

Space for calculation

average __________ **1**

(*b*) How many times greater was the pilot whale catch in 1996 than in 1994?

Space for calculation

__________ times **1**

[Turn over

DO NOT WRITE IN THIS MARGIN

Marks

7. Feather colour in parrots is controlled by a single gene. Blue feather colour (B) is dominant to yellow feather colour (b).

(*a*) A homozygous blue parrot is crossed with a homozygous yellow parrot.

(i) Complete the genotypes of the P generation.

P phenotype blue X yellow

P genotype __________ __________ **1**

(ii) State the genotype of the F_1 parrots.

F_1 genotype __________ **1**

(iii) State the phenotype of the F_1 parrots.

F_1 phenotype __________ **1**

(*b*) An F_1 individual is crossed with a true breeding yellow parrot.

Complete the punnet square to show the expected results of this cross.

Genotype of gametes from F_1 parent

Genotype of gametes from yellow parent		

2

DO NOT WRITE IN THIS MARGIN

Marks

8. (*a*) In African grasslands impala, giraffe and zebra feed on *Acacia* trees. Impala and zebra also graze on grasses.

Acacia

impala

giraffe

zebra

(i) State one way that competition for food is reduced between zebras and giraffes.

____ 1

(ii) The *Acacia* tree is adapted to withstand long periods of drought.

Suggest an adaptation the *Acacia* tree may show that allows it to survive long, dry periods.

____ 1

(*b*) In Scottish grasslands, sheep are often found as grazers. A very large flock of sheep was introduced into an area of ungrazed grassland.

Explain why this would decrease biodiversity within this area.

____

____ 2

[Turn over

DO NOT WRITE IN THIS MARGIN

Marks

9. The diagram below shows a section through a human heart.

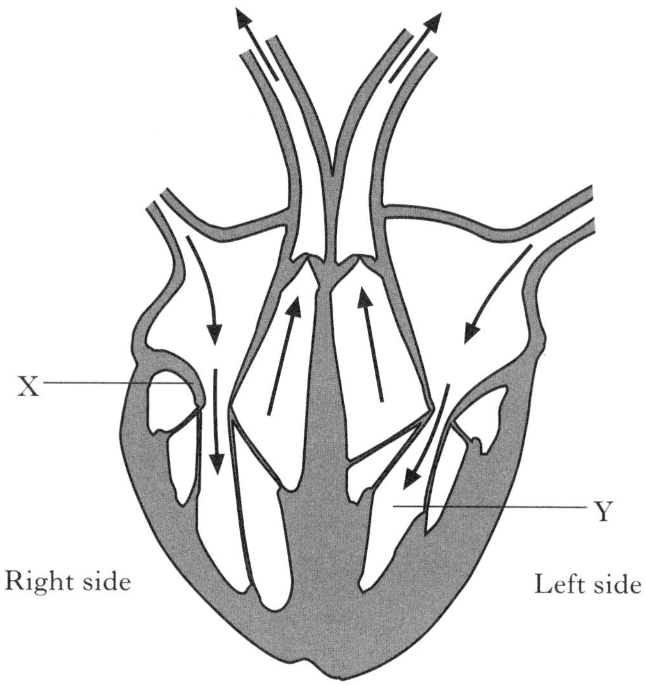

(*a*) Name valve X and chamber Y shown in the diagram.

X ______________________________

Y ______________________________ **1**

(*b*) Decide if each of the following statements about blood vessels is **True** or **False**, and tick (✓) the appropriate box.

If the statement is **False**, write the correct word in the **Correction** box to replace the word(s) underlined in the statement.

Statement	*True*	*False*	*Correction*
<u>Capillaries</u> contain valves.			
<u>Veins</u> allow gas exchange.			
Blood leaves the heart in <u>arteries</u>.			

3

DO NOT WRITE IN THIS MARGIN

Marks

9. (continued)

(*c*) The sentences below describe some of the functions of blood cells.

Underline one option in each set of brackets to make the sentences correct.

Oxygen is transported by {red / white} blood cells.

It combines with haemoglobin to form oxyhaemoglobin at {low / high} oxygen levels. **1**

Antibodies are produced by {macrophages / lymphocytes} **1**

[Turn over

DO NOT WRITE IN THIS MARGIN

Marks

10. The chart below shows the temperature of a patient over a 5 day period. Readings were taken daily at 7am and 7pm.

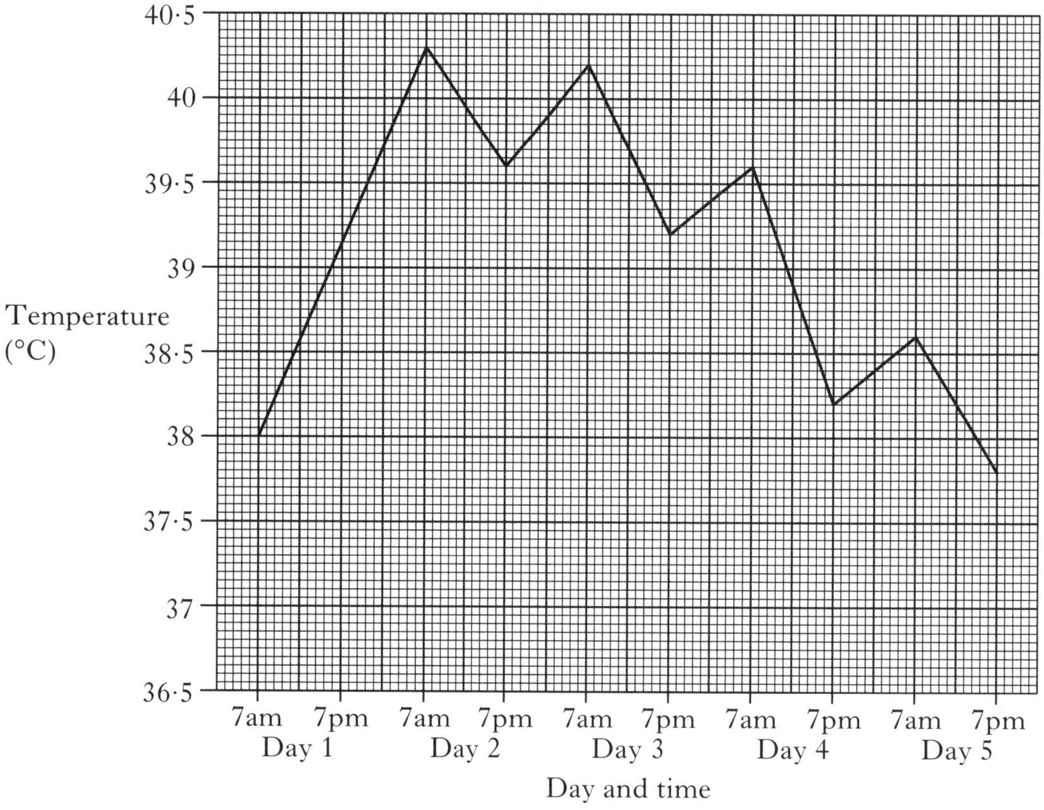

(*a*) (i) Calculate the temperature increase from 7am on Day 1 to 7am on Day 2.

Space for working

________ °C **1**

(ii) State **two** responses made by the body to cause the change in temperature observed on Day 2 from 7am to 7pm.

1. ______________________________

2. ______________________________ **2**

DO NOT WRITE IN THIS MARGIN

Marks

10. (continued)

(*b*) (i) Name the area of the brain containing the temperature regulating centre.

______________________ **1**

(ii) What term is used to describe the type of control mechanism which returns the body temperature to normal?

______________________ **1**

(iii) Describe how information is carried from temperature receptors in the skin to the brain.

______________________ **1**

[Turn over

DO NOT WRITE IN THIS MARGIN

Marks

11. The diagram below shows the human urinary system with its blood supply.

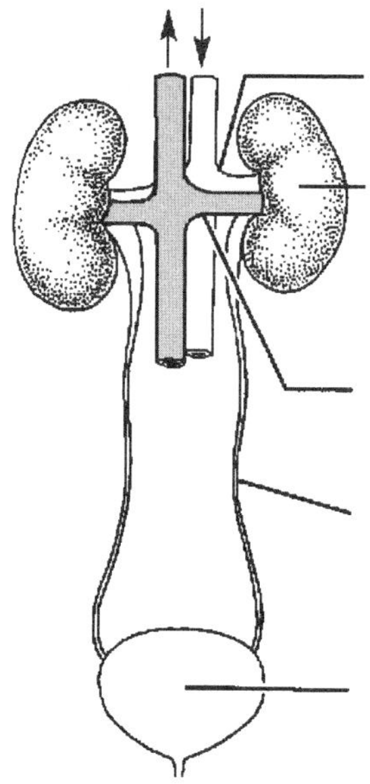

(*a*) An investigation was carried out to measure the concentration of three substances in samples of blood and urine.

The table below shows the results of this investigation.

Sample site	*Concentration* (grams per litre)		
	Glucose	*Urea*	*Salts*
Renal artery	1·0	0·3	8·0
Renal vein	0·8	0·0	6·0
Ureter	0·0	20·0	15·0

(i) Calculate the percentage of glucose remaining in the blood after it passes through the kidney.

Space for calculation

_______________% **1**

(ii) Explain how the data in the table supports the statement that urea is a waste product.

____

____ **1**

(iii) Name one substance, not shown in the table, which is present in urine.

_______________________ **1**

DO NOT WRITE IN THIS MARGIN

Marks

11. (continued)

(*b*) Name the two processes in the kidney which cause the differences in salt concentration between blood and urine.

Process 1 ______________________ **1**

Process 2 ______________________ **1**

(*c*) Freshwater bony fish use their kidneys to overcome a water balance problem.

Describe this problem and **one** method used by the kidneys to overcome it.

Problem ______________________ **1**

Method ______________________ **1**

[Turn over

DO NOT WRITE IN THIS MARGIN

Marks

12. (*a*) The diagram below shows the small intestine with associated organs and blood vessels.

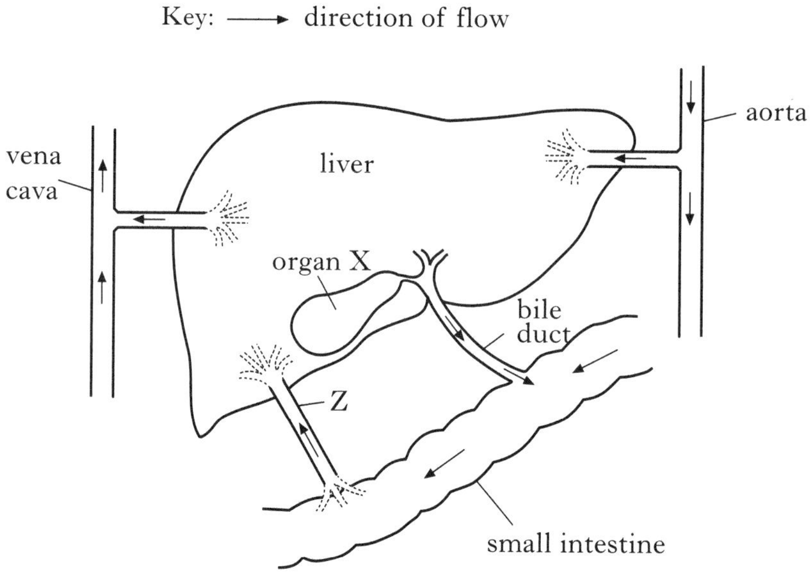

(i) Blood vessel Z carries amino acids to the liver.

(A) Name blood vessel Z.

______________________________ 1

(B) Describe what happens to excess amino acids in the liver.

______________________________ 1

(ii) (A) Name organ X.

______________________________ 1

(B) Describe the function of the bile that is released from organ X.

______________________________ 1

(*b*) Complete the table below which shows the substrate and product of two enzymes found in the small intestine.

Enzyme	*Substrate*	*Product*
	protein	
amylase		maltose

2

[Turn over for Section C on *page twenty-eight*

DO NOT WRITE IN THIS MARGIN

SECTION C

Both questions in this section should be attempted.

Note that each question contains a choice.

Questions 1 and 2 should be attempted on the blank pages which follow. All answers must be written clearly and legibly in ink.

Supplementary sheets, if required, may be obtained from the invigilator.

Marks

1. Answer **either** A **or** B.

A. The diagram below shows a section through a flower.

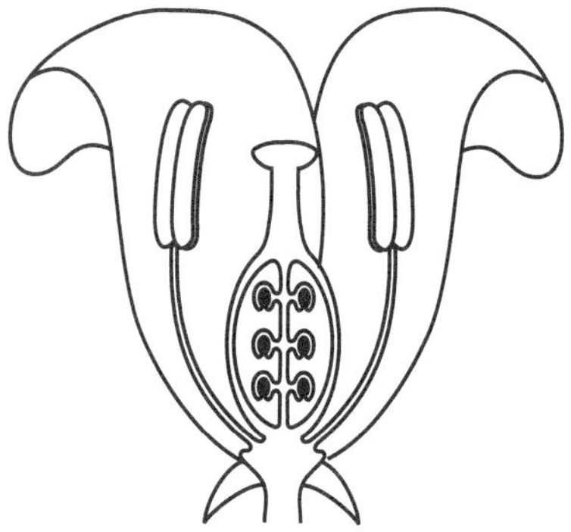

Name the sites of production of pollen grains and ovules in a flower. Describe how these gametes are formed and describe the process of fertilisation. **5**

OR

B. The diagram below summarises a form of genetic engineering.

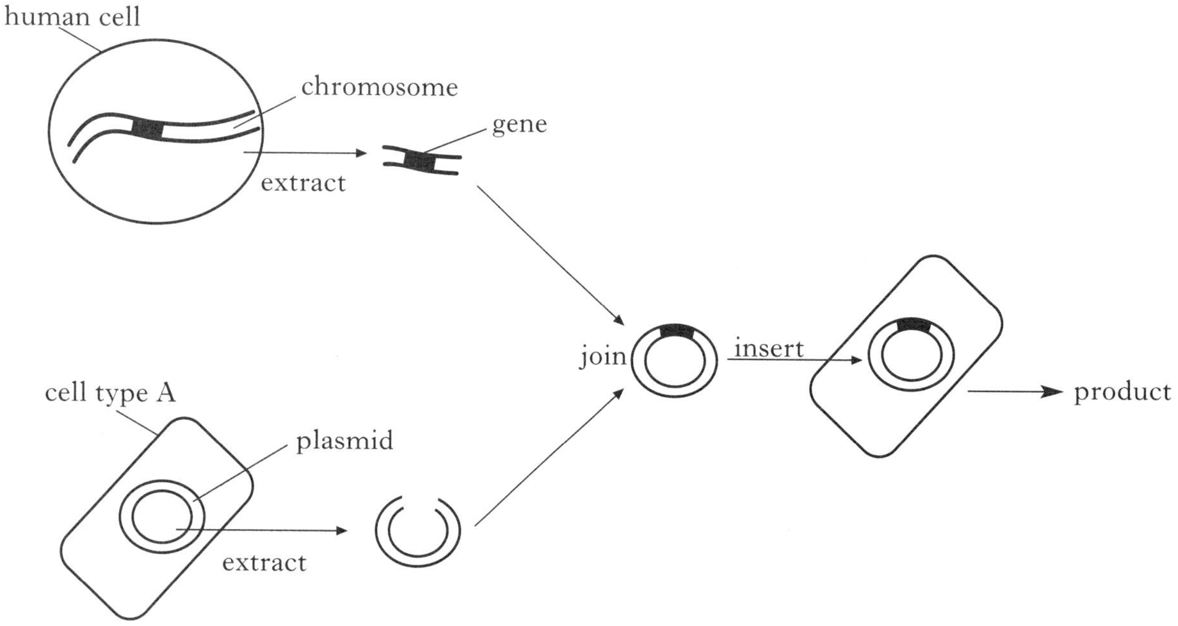

Identify cell type A and name a product of genetic engineering. Describe the advantages and disadvantages of this process. **5**

Question 2 is on *Page thirty*.

DO NOT WRITE IN THIS MARGIN

SPACE FOR ANSWER TO QUESTION 1

[Turn over for Question 2 on *Page thirty*

DO NOT WRITE IN THIS MARGIN

Marks

2. Answer **either** A **or** B.

Labelled diagrams may be included where appropriate.

A. Describe the function of yeast in bread making and the anaerobic pathway of respiration involved in this process. **5**

OR

B. Describe the properties of enzymes and the function of the enzyme phosphorylase in a synthesis reaction. **5**

[*END OF QUESTION PAPER*]

DO NOT WRITE IN THIS MARGIN

SPACE FOR ANSWER TO QUESTION 2

DO NOT WRITE IN THIS MARGIN

ADDITIONAL SPACE FOR ANSWERS

ADDITIONAL GRAPH PAPER FOR QUESTION 6(*a*)(i)

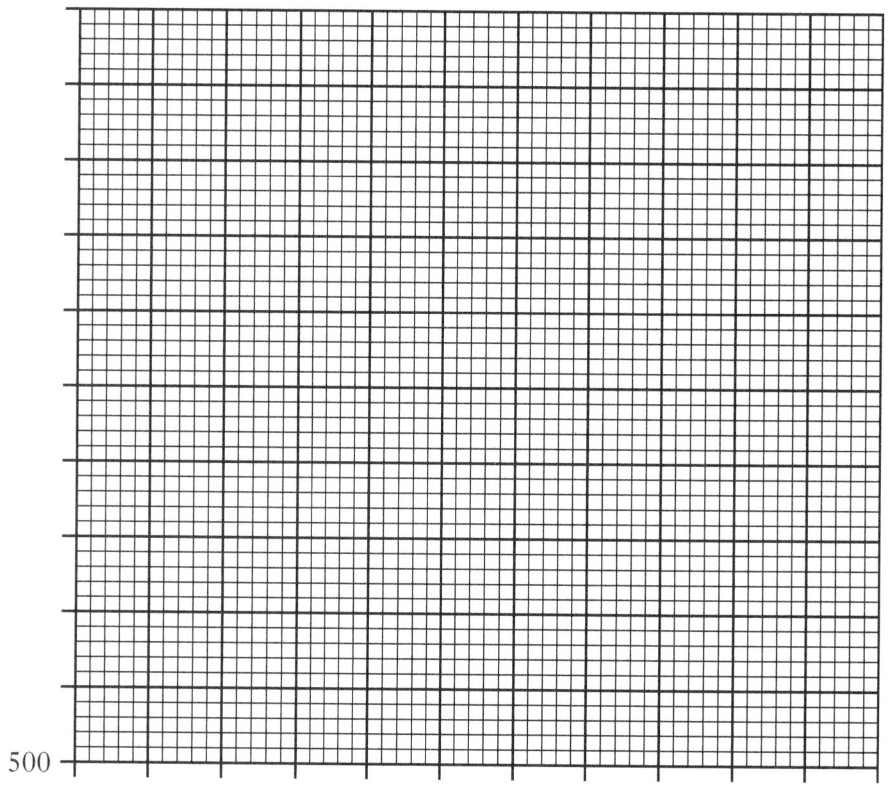

DO NOT WRITE IN THIS MARGIN

ADDITIONAL SPACE FOR ANSWERS

DO NOT WRITE IN THIS MARGIN

ADDITIONAL SPACE FOR ANSWERS

INTERMEDIATE 2

2009

[BLANK PAGE]

FOR OFFICIAL USE

Total for Sections B and C

X007/201

NATIONAL QUALIFICATIONS 2009

THURSDAY, 28 MAY
9.00 AM – 11.00 AM

BIOLOGY
INTERMEDIATE 2

Fill in these boxes and read what is printed below.

Full name of centre

Town

Forename(s)

Surname

Date of birth
Day Month Year

Scottish candidate number

Number of seat

SECTION A (25 marks)

Instructions for completion of Section A are given on page two.

For this section of the examination you must use an HB pencil.

SECTIONS B AND C (75 marks)

1 (a) All questions should be attempted.

(b) It should be noted that in **Section C** questions 1 and 2 each contain a choice.

2 The questions may be answered in any order but all answers are to be written in the spaces provided in this answer book, **and must be written clearly and legibly in ink**.

3 Additional space for answers will be found at the end of the book. If further space is required, supplementary sheets may be obtained from the invigilator and should be inserted inside the **front** cover of this book.

4 The numbers of questions must be clearly inserted with any answers written in the additional space.

5 Rough work, if any should be necessary, should be written in this book and then scored through when the fair copy has been written. If further space is required, a supplementary sheet for rough work may be obtained from the invigilator.

6 Before leaving the examination room you must give this book to the invigilator. If you do not, you may lose all the marks for this paper.

Read carefully

1 Check that the answer sheet provided is for **Biology Intermediate 2 (Section A)**.

2 For this section of the examination you must use an **HB pencil** and, where necessary, an eraser.

3 Check that the answer sheet you have been given has **your name**, **date of birth**, **SCN** (Scottish Candidate Number) and **Centre Name** printed on it.

Do not change any of these details.

4 If any of this information is wrong, tell the Invigilator immediately.

5 If this information is correct, **print** your name and seat number in the boxes provided.

6 The answer to each question is **either** A, B, C or D. Decide what your answer is, then, using your pencil, put a horizontal line in the space provided (see sample question below).

7 There is **only one correct** answer to each question.

8 Any rough working should be done on the question paper or the rough working sheet, **not** on your answer sheet.

9 At the end of the exam, put the **answer sheet for Section A inside the front cover of this answer book**.

Sample Question

Plants compete mainly for

A water, light and soil nutrients

B water, food and soil nutrients

C light, water and food

D light, food and soil nutrients.

The correct answer is **A**—water, light and soil nutrients. The answer **A** has been clearly marked in **pencil** with a horizontal line (see below).

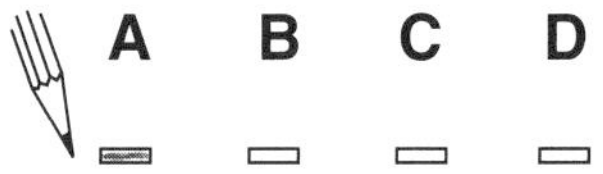

Changing an answer

If you decide to change your answer, carefully erase your first answer and using your pencil, fill in the answer you want. The answer below has been changed to **D**.

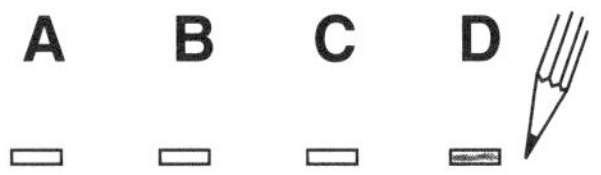

SECTION A

All questions in this Section should be attempted.

1. The diagram below shows a cell.

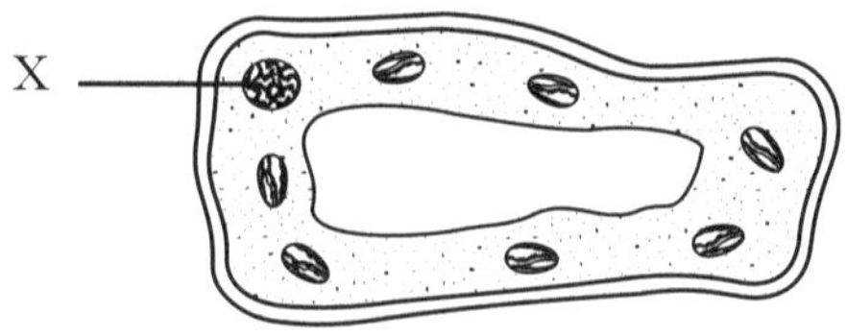

The function of structure X is to

A control cell activities

B keep the cell turgid

C control entry and exit of material

D release energy from glucose.

2. Fungi destroy bacteria by producing

A antibiotics

B alcohol

C carbon dioxide

D biogas.

3. The graph below shows the effect of temperature on the activity of the enzyme pepsin.

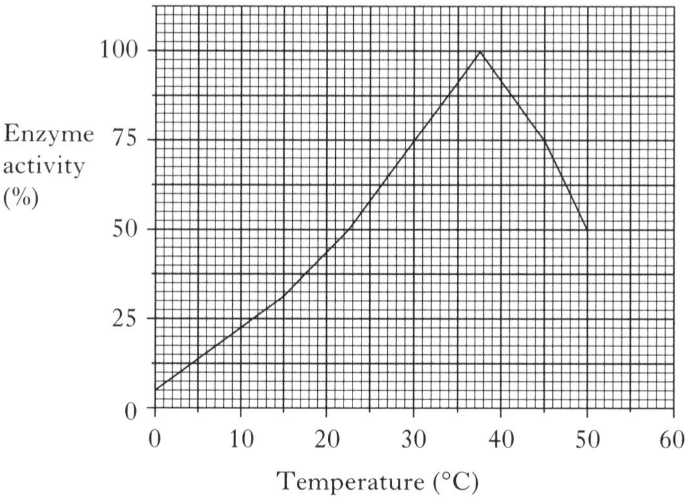

Between which two temperatures is there the greatest increase in enzyme activity?

A 0 – 10 °C

B 10 – 20 °C

C 20 – 30 °C

D 30 – 40 °C

4. In an investigation into the synthesis of starch from glucose-1-phosphate (G-1-P) by the enzyme phosphorylase, a tile was set up as shown below. Starch-free potato extract was used as the source of phosphorylase.

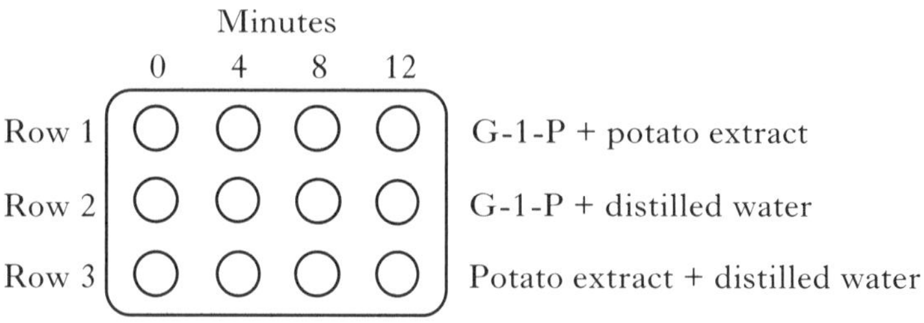

Iodine solution was added to the columns at the time intervals shown.

Which of the following tiles shows the expected result of this investigation?

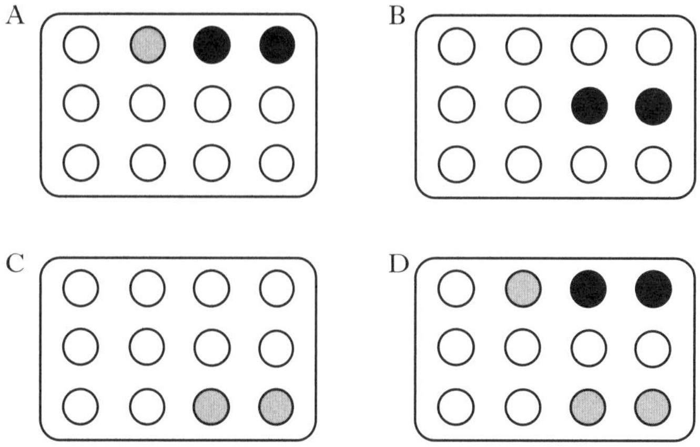

[Turn over

5. An investigation was carried out to measure the rate of carbon dioxide production in bread dough.

Carbon dioxide production was measured by recording the change in volume of a sample of bread dough over a 50 minute period.

The results are shown in the table below.

Time (minutes)	0	10	20	30	40	50
Volume of dough (cm^3)	10	14	18	21	23	25

The conclusion for this investigation was

A $0{\cdot}3\,cm^3$ of carbon dioxide was produced per minute

B $0{\cdot}5\,cm^3$ of carbon dioxide was produced per minute

C $15\,cm^3$ of carbon dioxide was produced per minute

D $25\,cm^3$ of carbon dioxide was produced per minute.

6. The apparatus below was used to investigate respiration in germinating peas.

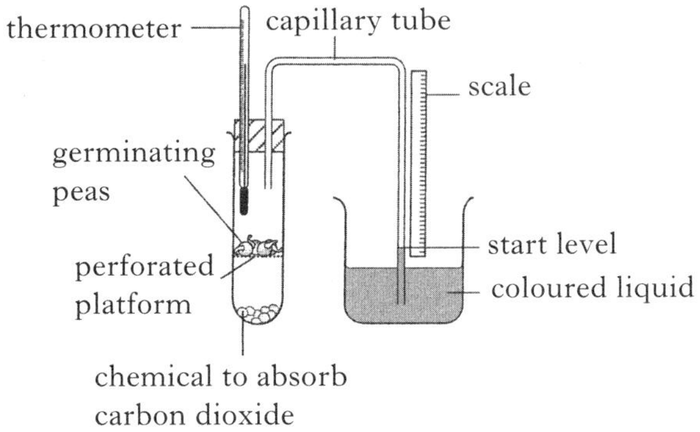

A suitable control for this investigation would be

A

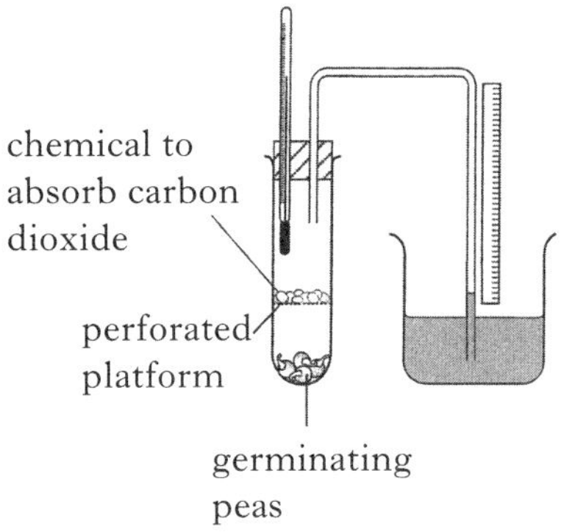

B

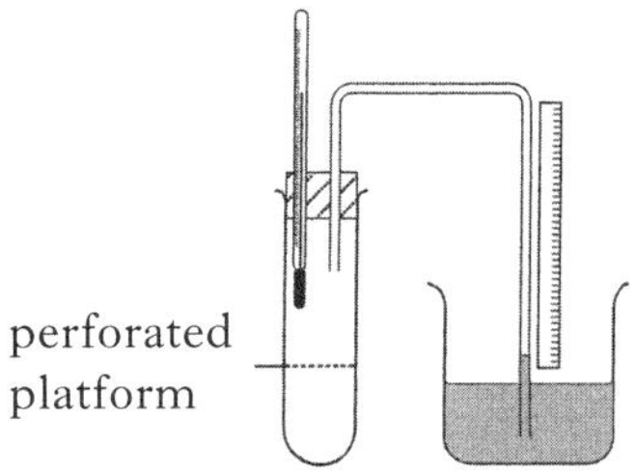

C

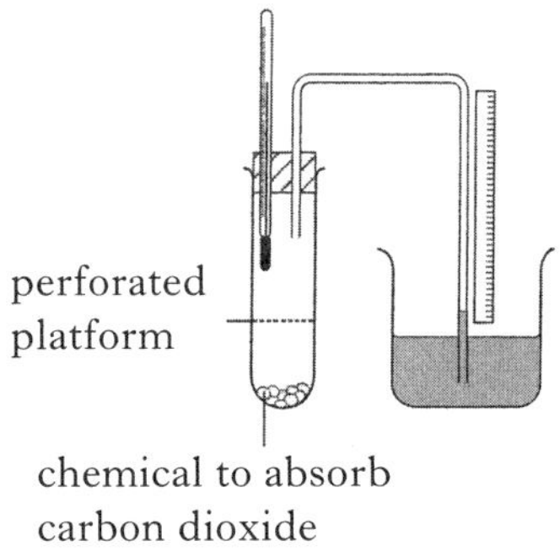

D

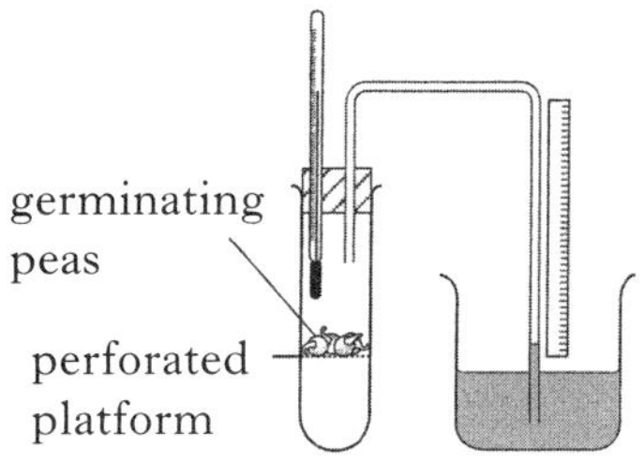

7. The graph shows the effect of varying the light intensity, temperature and carbon dioxide concentration on the rate of photosynthesis.

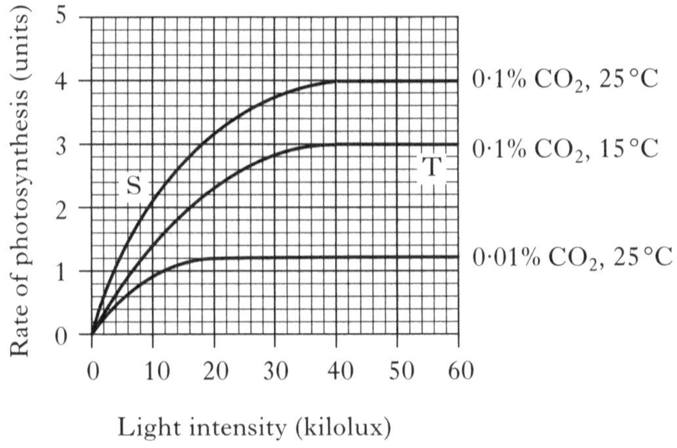

The rate of photosynthesis is being limited by

A temperature at S and light intensity at T

B light intensity at S and temperature at T

C carbon dioxide at S and temperature at T

D light intensity at S and carbon dioxide at T.

8. Which of the following conditions in a greenhouse would produce earlier crops?

A Glass shading

B Cool air conditioners

C Additional oxygen

D Additional carbon dioxide

9. The diagram below shows part of a food chain in the Arctic tundra.

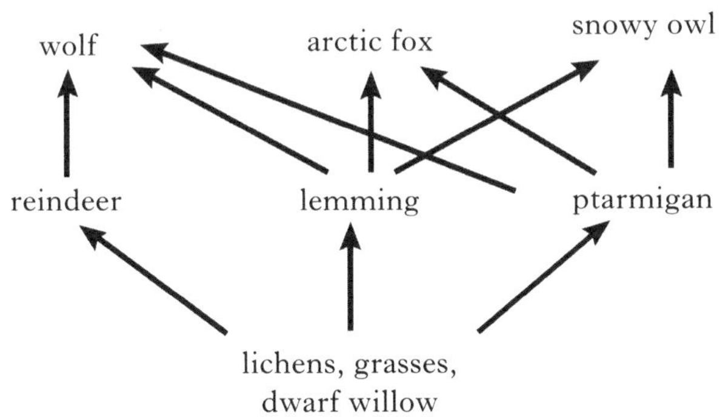

A population in this food web is all the

A plants

B reindeer

C animals

D living organisms.

10. The diagram below represents a field (Y) with an area (X) fenced off.

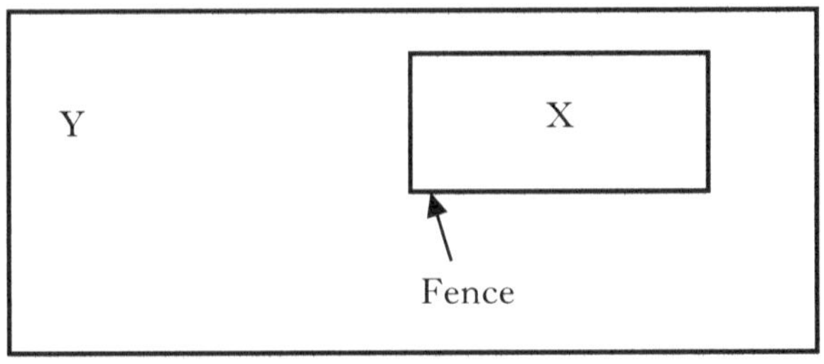

Sheep and rabbits provide very high intensity of grazing in area Y but cannot graze in fenced off area X.

Which line in the table below describes the diversity of plant species in areas X and Y after one year?

	Diversity of plant species	
	Area X	*Area Y*
A	higher	lower
B	lower	higher
C	higher	higher
D	lower	lower

11. The chromosome complement of a human individual who inherits an X-chromosome from their father is

A 44 including XX

B 44 including XY

C 46 including XX

D 46 including XY

[Turn over

12. In humans, the allele for free earlobes (E) is dominant to the allele for fixed earlobes (e).

The diagram below shows the inheritance of this characteristic.

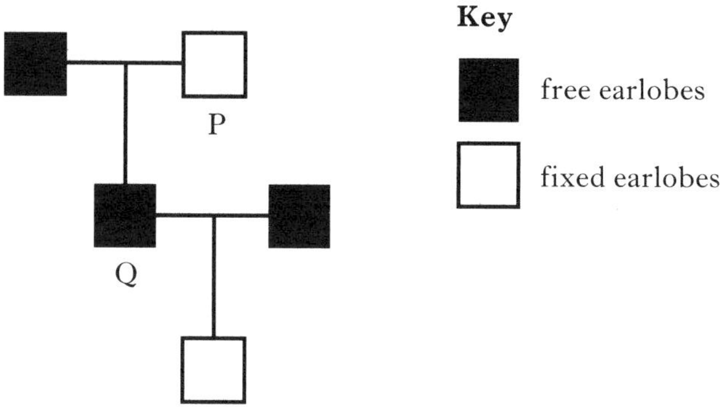

Which line in the table identifies correctly the genotypes of persons P and Q?

	Genotype	
	P	*Q*
A	ee	EE
B	ee	Ee
C	EE	Ee
D	Ee	Ee

13. A hairy stemmed pea plant was crossed with a smooth stemmed pea plant and all of the F_1 had hairy stems.

The genotype of the hairy stemmed parent plant is

A heterozygous dominant

B heterozygous recessive

C homozygous recessive

D homozygous dominant.

14. In gerbils, agouti coat colour is dominant to white.

Some heterozygous gerbils were allowed to interbreed and 56 offspring were produced. What would be the expected number of agouti gerbils?

A 14

B 28

C 42

D 56

15. Skin colour in humans is an example of

A discontinuous variation

B co-dominance

C polygenic inheritance

D random assortment.

16. The diagram below shows stages in the production of a desired product by genetic engineering.

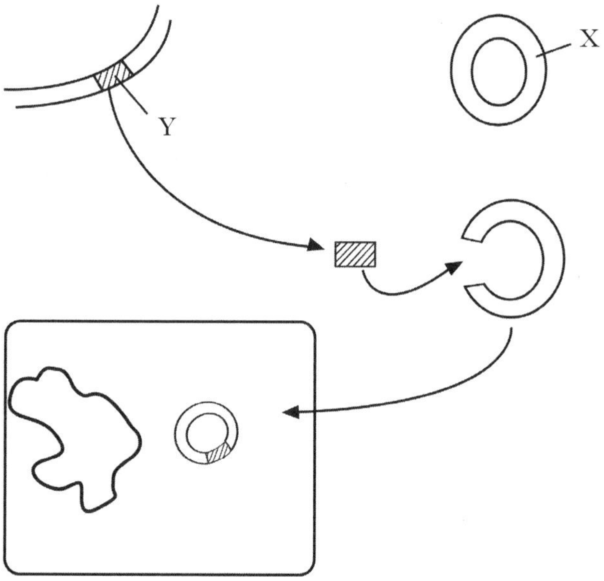

Which line in the table identifies correctly the structures labelled above?

	X	*Y*
A	bacterium	gene
B	plasmid	chromosome
C	bacterium	chromosome
D	plasmid	gene

17. Digestion takes place in animals

A and allows insoluble molecules to pass directly through the wall of the small intestine

B as enzymes cannot act on insoluble molecules

C and makes insoluble molecules into soluble molecules to allow absorption

D and allows food to be passed along the gut by peristalsis.

18. Salivary glands produce mucus to

A lubricate the food in the stomach

B lubricate the food to aid swallowing

C protect the mouth from amylase

D protect the oesophagus from amylase.

19. In the stomach, proteins are broken down into polypeptides.

The graph below shows the concentrations of protein and polypeptides in the stomach over 40 minutes.

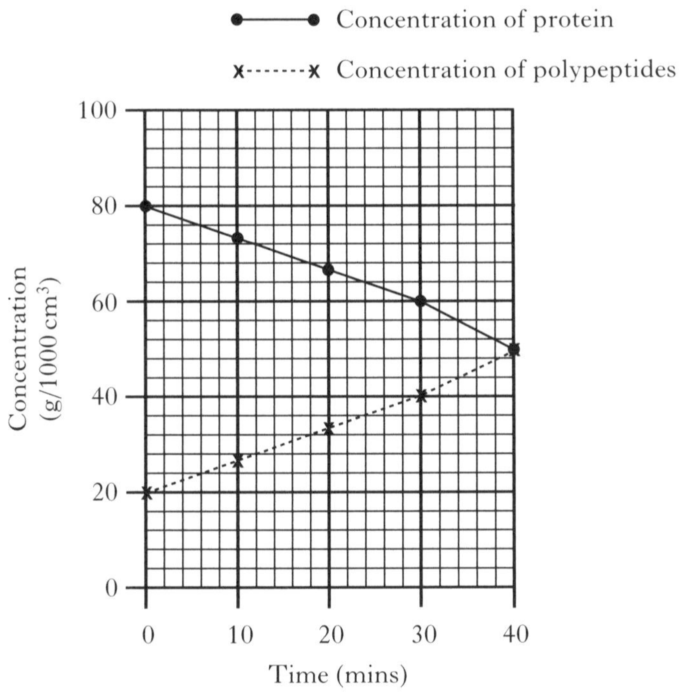

What was the ratio of protein concentration to polypeptide concentration after 30 minutes?

A 3 : 2

B 2 : 3

C 2 : 1

D 1 : 2

20. The diagram below shows some structures in a villus.

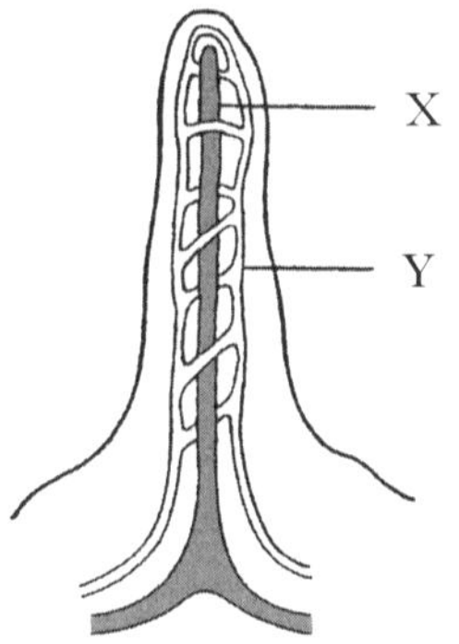

Which line in the table below correctly identifies the products of digestion which pass into structures X and Y?

	X	*Y*
A	glucose	amino acids
B	glycerol	fatty acids
C	amino acids	glycogen
D	fatty acids	glucose

21. Which line in the table identifies correctly the functions of the large intestine and the anus?

	Large intestine	*Anus*
A	digests food material	eliminates undigested material
B	stores undigested material	absorbs water from undigested material
C	absorbs water from undigested material	eliminates undigested material
D	absorbs digested food products	absorbs water from undigested material

22. The diagram below shows the human urinary system.

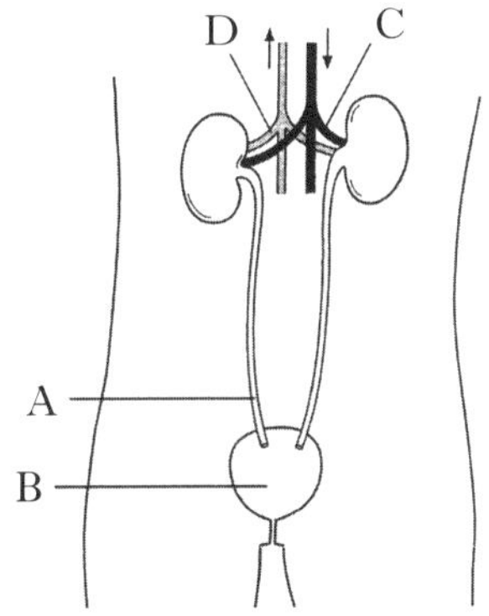

Which labelled part is the ureter?

23. The graph below shows the results of an investigation on the effect of ADH on urine production.

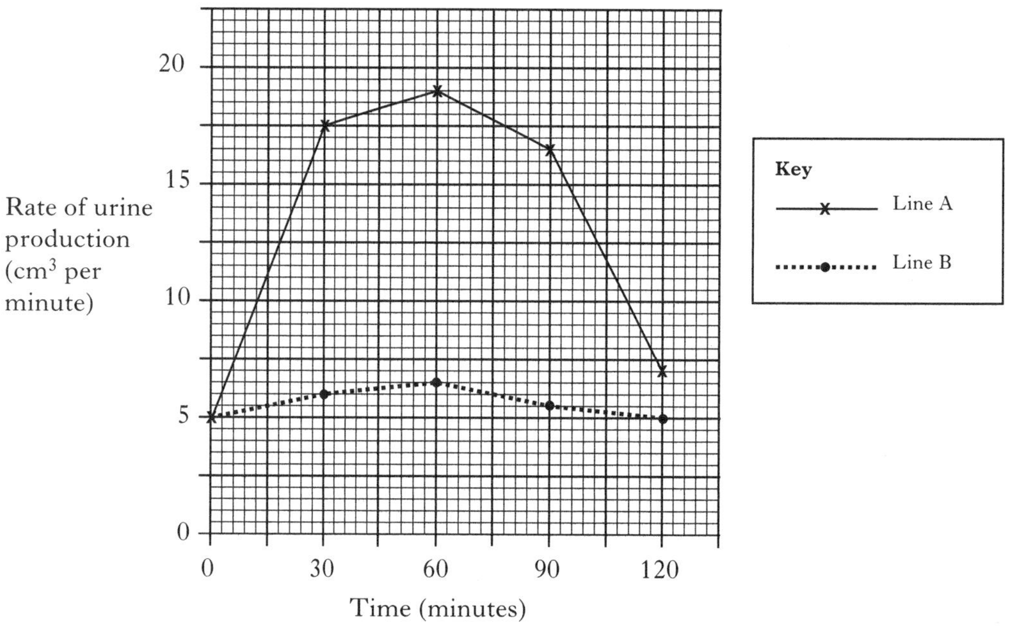

Line A shows the rate of urine production for a volunteer after drinking one litre of water.

Line B shows the rate of urine production from the same volunteer after drinking one litre of water and receiving an injection of ADH.

After 60 minutes, what was the difference between the rates of urine production with and without the ADH injection?

A 6·5 cm^3 per minute

B 12·5 cm^3 per minute

C 19·0 cm^3 per minute

D 25·5 cm^3 per minute

24. The diagram below shows an air sac with part of its capillary network.

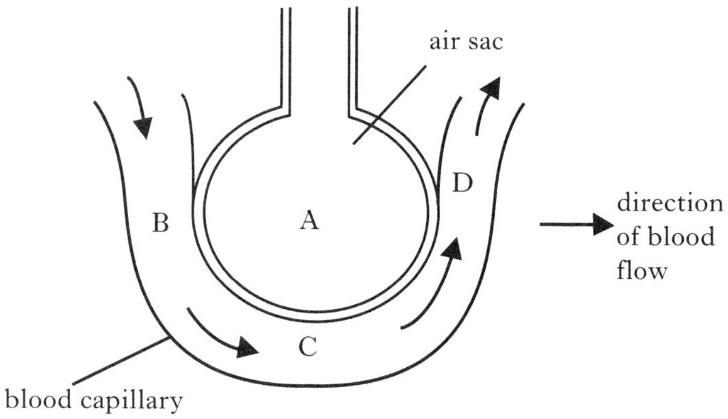

At which position would blood with the highest concentration of oxygen be found?

25. The diagram below shows a section through the human brain.

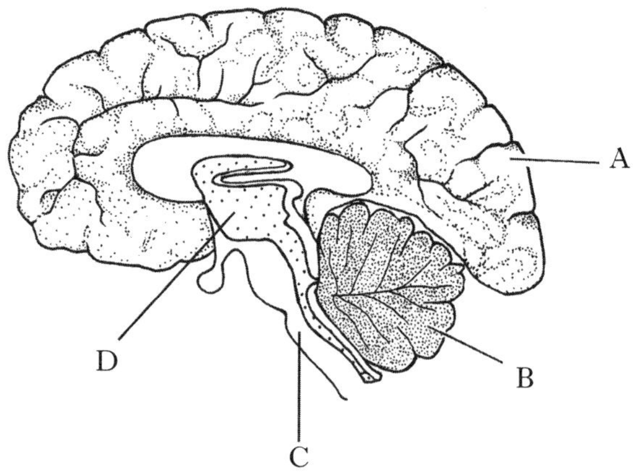

Which labelled part is the site of temperature regulation?

Candidates are reminded that the answer sheet for Section A MUST be placed INSIDE the front cover of this answer book.

DO NOT WRITE IN THIS MARGIN

SECTION B

All questions in this section should be attempted.
All answers must be written clearly and legibly in ink.

Marks

1. (*a*) The diagram below shows three stages X, Y and Z that occur when an enzyme converts its substrate into a product.

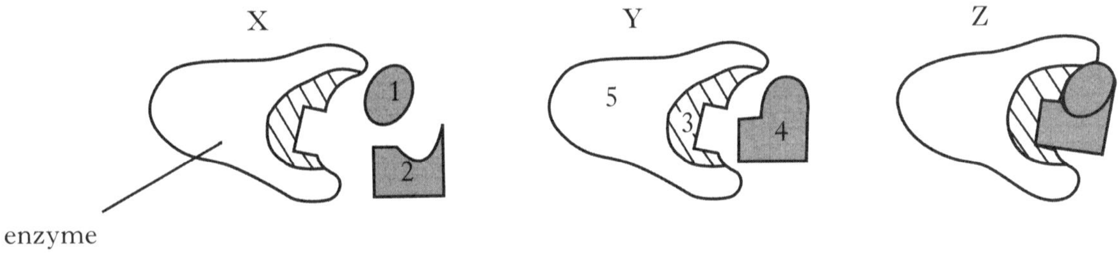

(i) This enzyme promotes the breakdown of a complex molecule into simpler molecules.

Put the stages into the correct order to show this degradation reaction.

________ → ________ → ________ **1**

(ii) Which number in the diagram shows the active site?

________ **1**

(*b*) Complete the following sentence by underlining the correct word from the choice in brackets.

Enzymes are made of { carbohydrate / fat / protein }. **1**

(*c*) Describe what happens to an enzyme when it is denatured.

____

________________________________ **1**

[Turn over

DO NOT WRITE IN THIS MARGIN

Marks

2. Liver contains the enzyme catalase which carries out the following reaction.

hydrogen peroxide ⟶ water + oxygen

The investigation shown below was carried out to demonstrate the effect of pH on catalase activity in liver.

Hydrogen peroxide of different pH values was added to 1 g of roughly chopped raw liver.

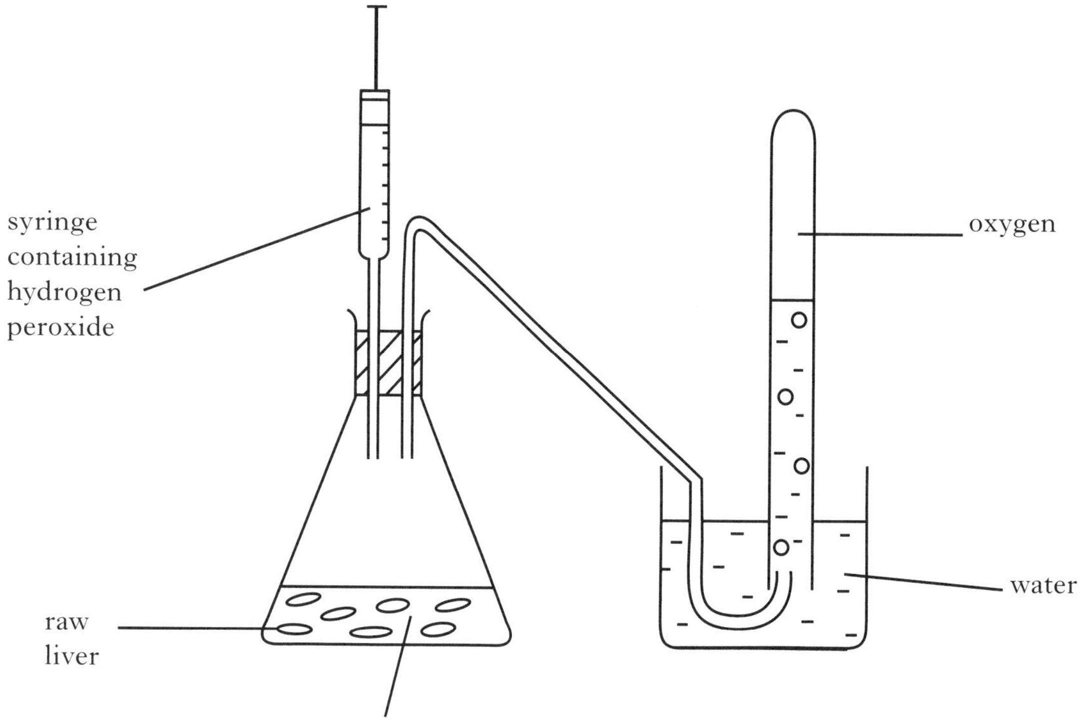

The time taken to collect 1cm^3 of oxygen was recorded and the results are shown in the table below.

pH of hydrogen peroxide solution	*Time to collect 1 cm^3 of oxygen* (seconds)			*Average time to collect 1cm^3 of oxygen* (seconds)
	Trial 1	*Trial 2*	*Trial 3*	
7	76	77	81	78
8	56	58	57	57
9	50	45	40	45
10	53	50	53	52
11	59	69	70	66

(*a*) From the table, state the optimum pH for catalase in liver.

________________ **1**

DO NOT WRITE IN THIS MARGIN

Marks

2. (continued)

(*b*) Name the variable altered in this investigation.

______________________________ 1

(*c*) Explain why the experiment was repeated at each pH value and averages calculated.

______________________________ 1

(*d*) Construct a line graph of the **average** time taken to collect 1 cm^3 of oxygen against pH of hydrogen peroxide solution.

(Additional graph paper, if required, will be found on *Page thirty-two*)

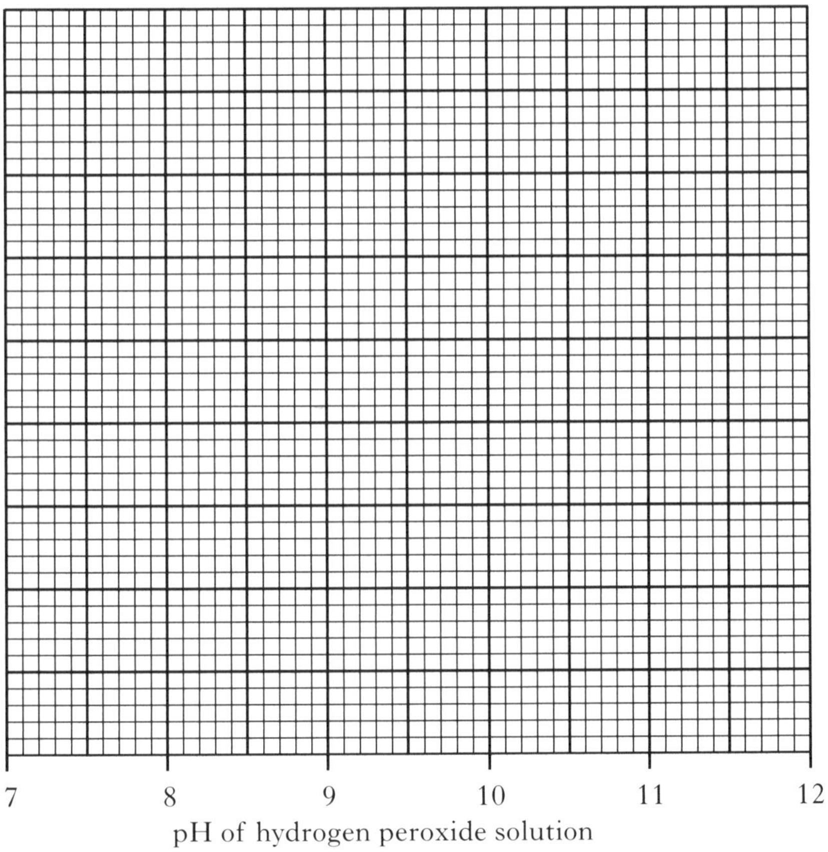

2

(*e*) Predict the average time to collect 1 cm^3 of oxygen at pH12.

______________ seconds 1

[Turn over

DO NOT WRITE IN THIS MARGIN

Marks

3. Yeast may carry out two different types of respiration.

(*a*) Name the type of respiration in yeast which has the highest energy yield.

_______________________ **1**

(*b*) The diagram below shows one type of respiration in yeast cells.

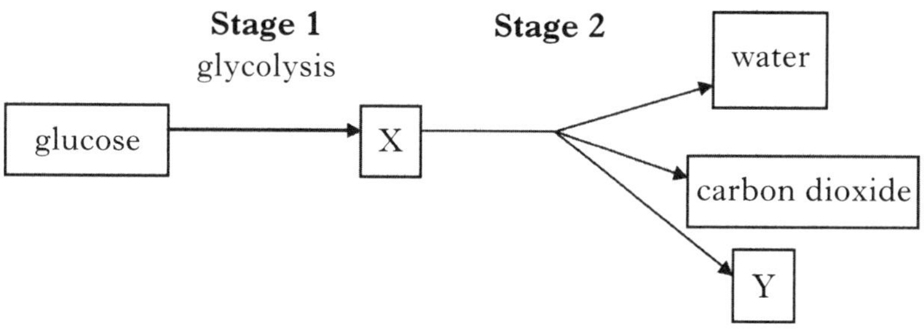

(i) Name substances X and Y.

X _______________________ **1**

Y _______________________ **1**

(ii) What other substance must be present for stage 2 to occur?

_______________________ **1**

(*c*) Yeast cells are used in the brewing industry.

(i) Name the type of respiration involved.

_______________________ **1**

(ii) Explain why yeast cells are used in the brewing industry.

_______________________ **1**

DO NOT WRITE IN THIS MARGIN

Marks

4. (*a*) The diagram below shows an investigation into the effect of adding three different solutions to three pieces of muscle tissue.

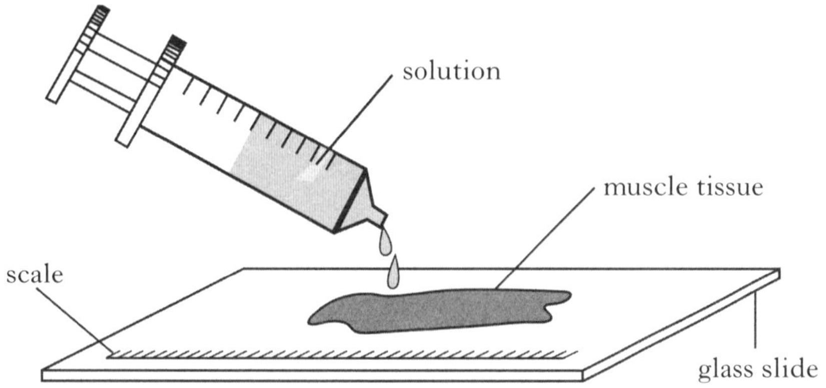

The results of the investigation are given in the table below.

Muscle tissue	*Solution added*	*Length of muscle tissue*			
		at start (mm)	*after 5 minutes* (mm)	*difference in length* (mm)	*percentage difference* (%)
1	1% glucose	50	50	0	0
2	1% ATP	45	41·5	4·5	10
3	0·5% ATP	48	45·6	2·4	

(i) Calculate the percentage difference in length for muscle tissue 3.

Space for calculation

____________ % **1**

(ii) What conclusion can be drawn from the results?

____

______________________________ **1**

(*b*) (i) What term is used to describe the effect of lactic acid build up in muscle tissue?

______________________________ **1**

(ii) How can lactic acid be removed from muscle tissue?

______________________________ **1**

Marks

5. (*a*) The diagram below represents a food chain in a garden.

(*The organisms are not to scale.*)

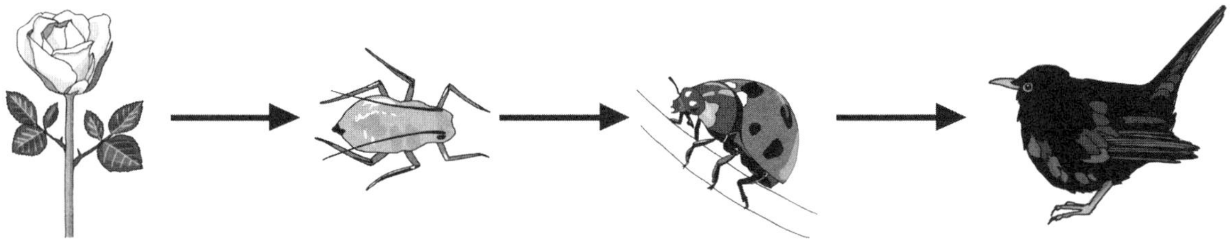

rose bush | greenfly | ladybird | blackbird

(i) What term describes the greenfly in this food chain?

____ **1**

(ii) A rose bush contains 10 000 kJ/m^2/year of energy and only 10% of this energy is passed on at each stage of the food chain.

Use this information to complete the pyramid of energy below for this food chain.

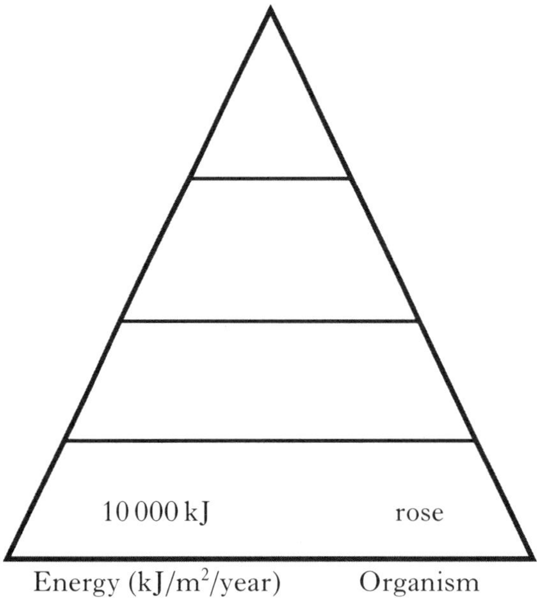

2

(iii) What happens to the energy that is **not** passed on at each stage of the food chain?

______________________________ **1**

(*b*) Many ladybirds were seen over the summer in the garden.

They were able to interbreed and produce fertile offspring.

What can be concluded about the ladybirds, using all this information?

____ **1**

DO NOT WRITE IN THIS MARGIN

Marks

6. The following table shows four blood groups and their frequency in a population.

Blood Group	*Frequency in population* (%)
O	44
A	42
B	10
AB	4

(*a*) Calculate the simplest whole number ratio of the frequency of blood groups O to AB.

Space for calculation

Blood group _____ : _____ **1**

O AB

(*b*) Name the type of variation shown by these blood groups.

______________________________ **1**

(*c*) Blood group is determined by three alleles A, B, O.

The table below shows the possible genotypes of each blood group.

Genotype	*Blood group*
OO	O
AO, AA	A
BO, BB	B
AB	AB

(i) Which of these alleles are co-dominant?

______________________________ **1**

(ii) Explain the meaning of co-dominant alleles.

____

____ **1**

DO NOT WRITE IN THIS MARGIN

Marks

7. (*a*) The diagram below shows a summary of events that occur during reproduction in a flowering plant.

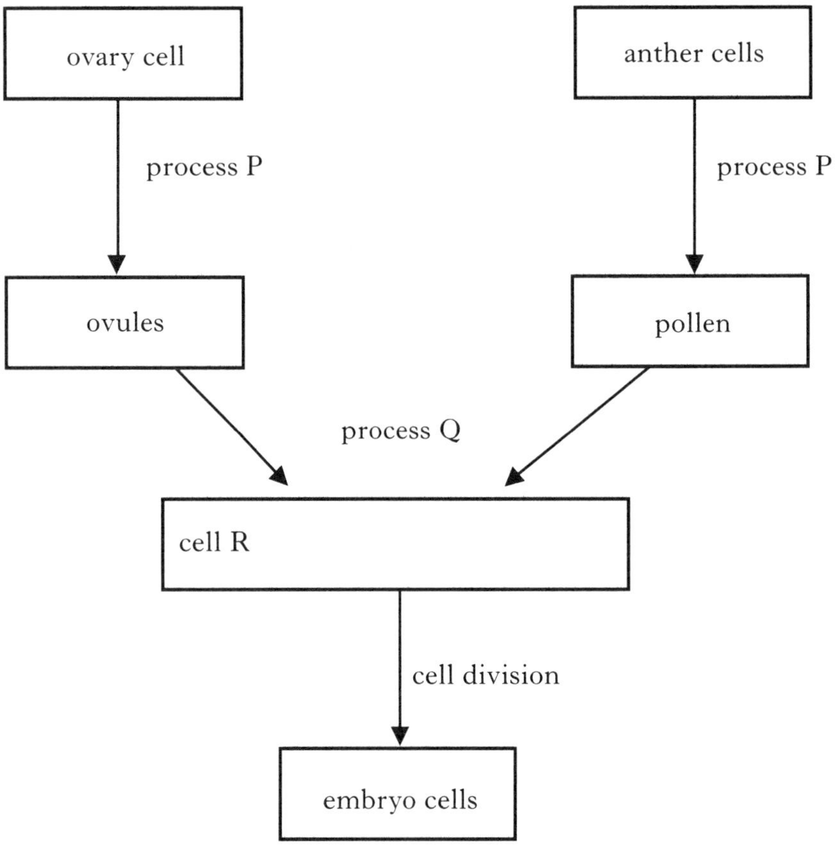

(i) **Complete the diagram** by entering the name of cell type R. **1**

(ii) Which process in the diagram represents fertilisation?

________________________________ **1**

(iii) Complete the following table by inserting a tick (✓) in the correct boxes to show which of the cells in the diagram have a double or single set of chromosomes.

Cell	*Double set of chromosomes*	*Single set of chromosomes*
anther		
ovule		
R		
embryo		

2

DO NOT WRITE IN THIS MARGIN

Marks

7. (continued)

(*b*) Explain the need to produce cells with a single set of chromosomes in reproduction.

____

____ **1**

(*c*) Underline one option in each set of brackets to make the following sentence correct.

Random assortment of chromosomes occurs during {meiosis / fertilisation} which {increases / decreases} the {biodiversity / variation} of gametes. **2**

[Turn over

Marks DO NOT WRITE IN THIS MARGIN

8. An investigation to demonstrate the responses of woodlice to light was carried out in a choice chamber. Half of the choice chamber was covered in black paper and the other half left in light.

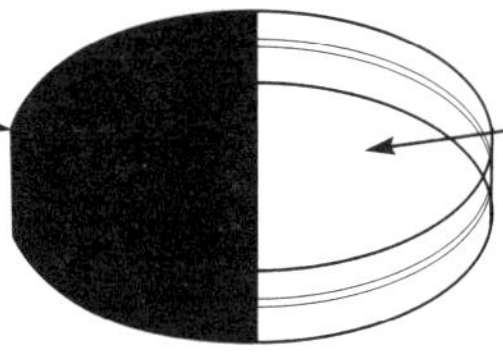

Ten woodlice were introduced into the choice chamber. The number of woodlice in each side was counted every two minutes for ten minutes.

The graph shows the results of this investigation.

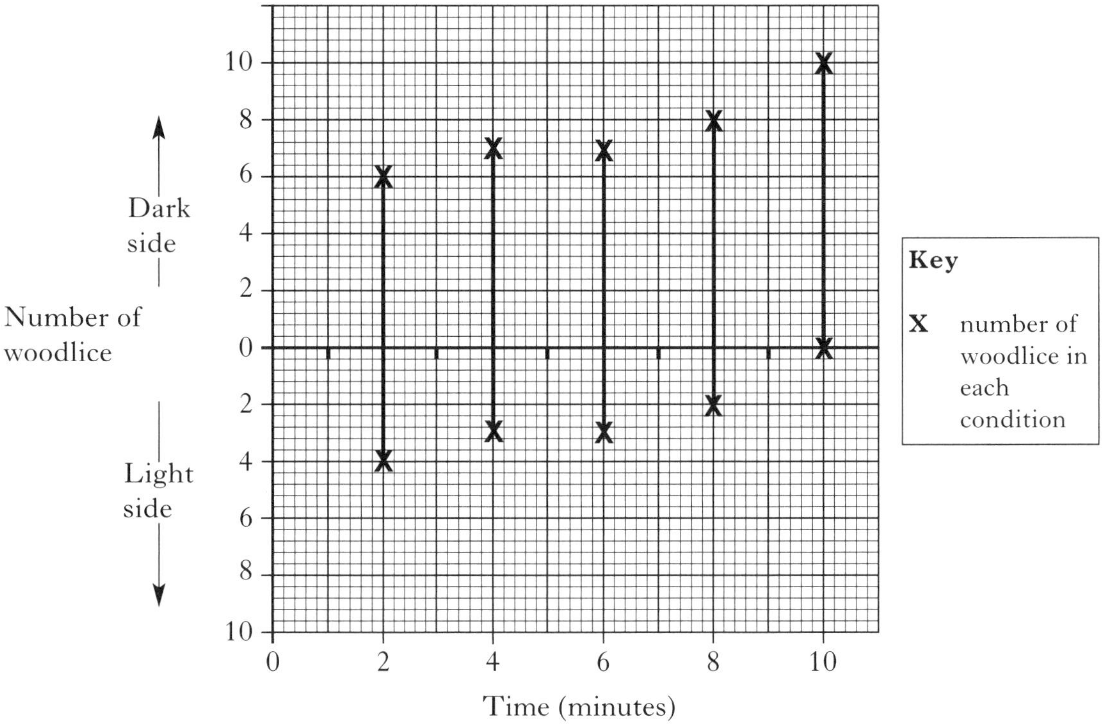

(*a*) Name two environmental conditions that should be kept constant in this investigation.

1 ______________________________

2 ______________________________ **2**

(*b*) What conclusion can be made from the results of this investigation?

____

______________________________ **1**

(*c*) Explain the advantage of this behaviour to the woodlice.

____

______________________________ **1**

DO NOT WRITE IN THIS MARGIN

Marks

9. It is thought that Darwin's finches evolved from one type of ancestral finch.

The diagram below shows examples of different species of Darwin's finches.

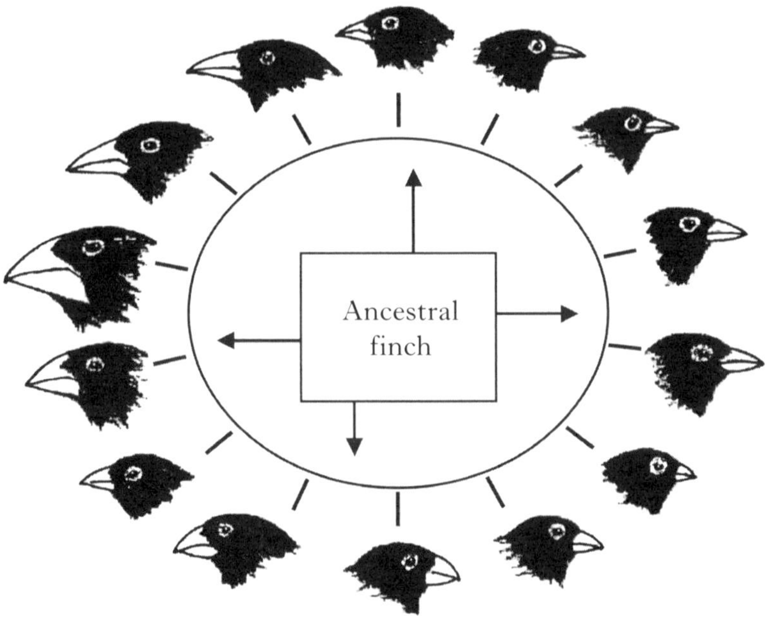

(*a*) (i) What **two** observations can be made from the diagram about the structure of the finches' beaks?

____ **1**

(ii) Name one environmental factor which has led to this variation.

____ **1**

(*b*) What term is used to describe the role that each finch plays within its community?

____ **1**

(*c*) The existence of some Darwin's finches is under threat in the Galapagos Islands due to human activity.

(i) Give an example of a human activity that could be affecting the finches.

____ **1**

(ii) What could be an effect of this human activity on finch biodiversity?

____ **1**

[Turn over

Marks

10. The diagram below shows a section through the heart.

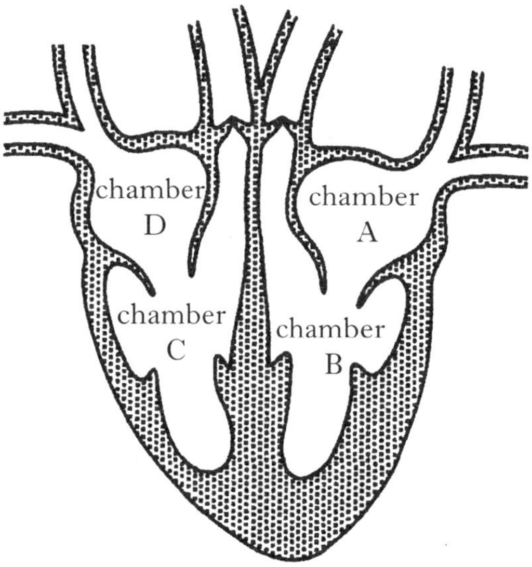

(*a*) (i) Blood follows a pathway through the heart and lungs from the vena cava to the aorta. Use letters from the diagram to complete the following flow chart to show the correct pathway.

vena cava → [ ] → [ ] → lungs → [ ] → [ ] → aorta **1**

(ii) State the letter of a chamber of the heart which contains oxygenated blood.

Chamber ________________ **1**

DO NOT WRITE IN THIS MARGIN

Marks

10. (continued)

(*b*) Decide if each of the following statements about the transport of gases by the bloodstream is **True** or **False**, and tick (✓) the appropriate box.

If the statement is **False** write the correct word in the **Correction box** to replace the word underlined in the statement.

Statement	*True*	*False*	*Correction*
Oxygen forms oxyhaemoglobin at low oxygen levels in the lungs.			
Carbon dioxide is transported in red blood cells.			
Carbon dioxide dissolved in the blood plasma decreases acidity.			

3

[Turn over

DO NOT WRITE IN THIS MARGIN

Marks

11. (*a*) An investigation was carried out to estimate the concentration of urea in two unknown urine samples. A tablet of the enzyme urease was added to a test tube containing the urine sample. When urease reacted with urea in the sample the gas produced turned moist litmus paper blue.

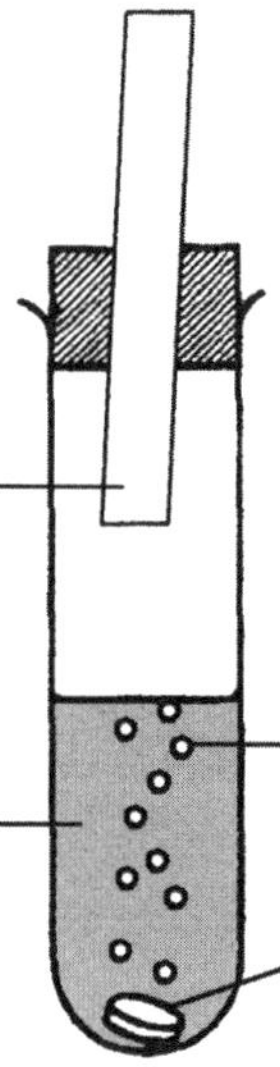

The time taken for the litmus paper to turn blue was recorded in each case.

The table below shows the results obtained when various urine samples of known and unknown urea concentration were tested.

Concentration of urea in urine sample ($g/100\,cm^3$)	*Time taken for litmus paper to turn blue* (seconds)
0·5	300
1·5	210
2·5	115
3·5	10
unknown A	75
unknown B	225

(i) Which unknown urine sample, A or B, has the lowest concentration of urea?

__________ **1**

(ii) Suggest a reason for a low concentration of urea in urine.

____ **1**

DO NOT WRITE IN THIS MARGIN

Marks

11. (*a*) (continued)

(iii) Predict the effect on the results if the temperature was increased from 20°C to 30°C in this investigation.

______________________________ 1

(iv) Describe a suitable control for this investigation.

______________________________ 1

(*b*) The diagram below shows the parts of a kidney nephron involved in filtration.

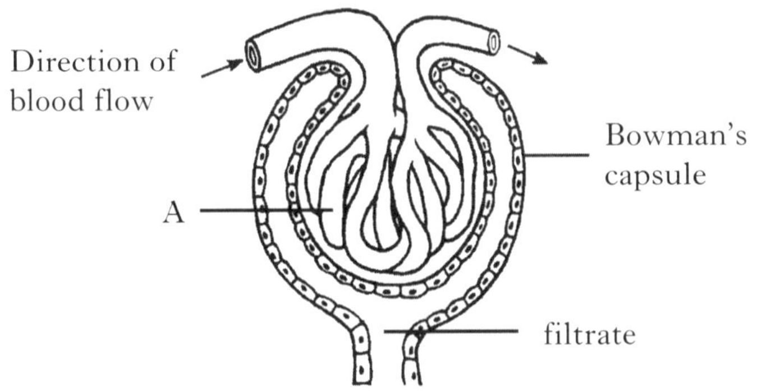

(i) Name part A which consists of a bundle of blood capillaries.

______________________________ 1

(ii) Describe the process which forms urine from the filtrate.

____

______________________________ 1

[Turn over

DO NOT WRITE IN THIS MARGIN

Marks

12. (*a*) The diagram below shows the human breathing system.

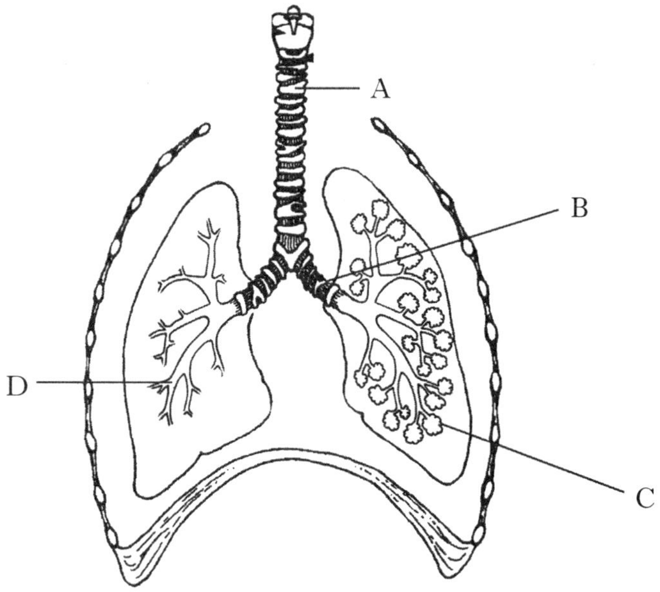

Complete the table below to identify the labelled structures.

Letter	*Name of structure*
	bronchiole
B	
	trachea
C	

2

DO NOT WRITE IN THIS MARGIN

Marks

12. (continued)

(*b*) A person breathed normally, took deep breaths, then returned to normal breathing.

The volume of air in the lungs was measured and the results are shown in the graph below.

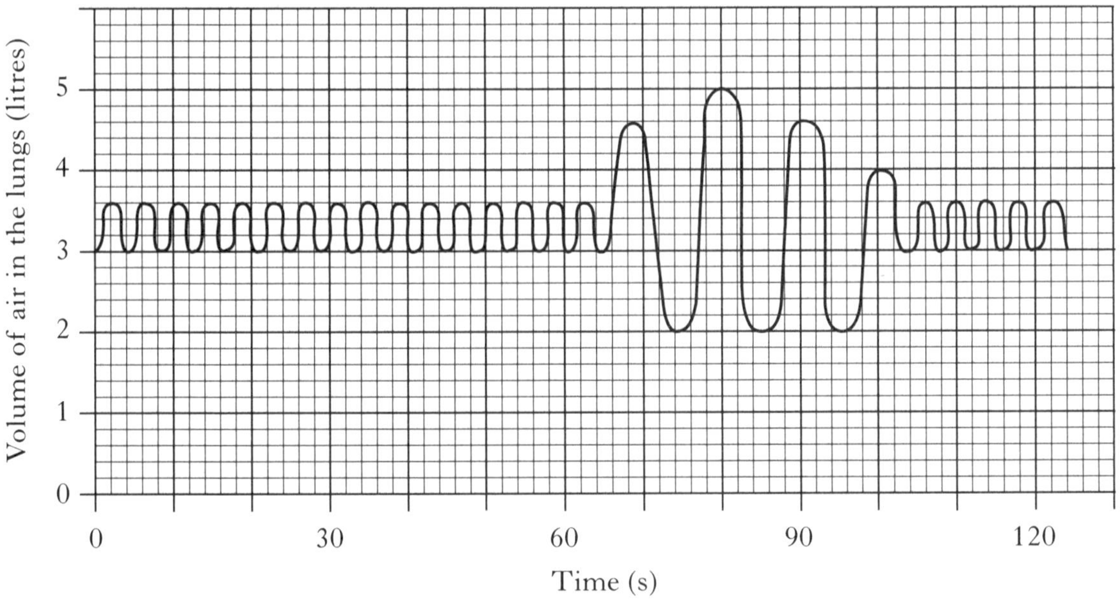

(i) What was the normal breathing rate for this person?

____________________ breaths per minute **1**

(ii) What was the highest volume of air inhaled in a single breath?

____________________ litres **1**

[Turn over

DO NOT WRITE IN THIS MARGIN

Marks

13. (*a*) The diagram below shows parts of the central nervous system (CNS) and a nerve to the heart.

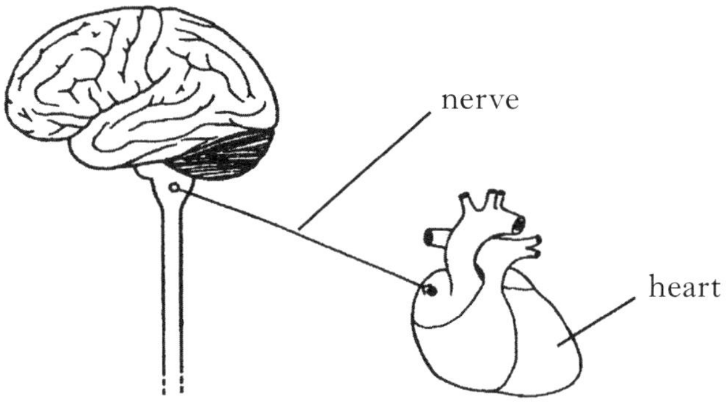

(i) Name the two parts, shown in the diagram, which make up the central nervous system (CNS).

1 ____________________

2 ____________________ **1**

(ii) Name the area, shown in the diagram, which controls heart rate.

________________________________ **1**

(*b*) Reflex arcs contain relay fibres.

(i) Which structure sends impulses to the relay fibre?

____ **1**

(ii) What is the function of relay fibres in a reflex arc?

____ **1**

(*c*) Explain the function of a reflex response.

____

____ **1**

[Turn over for Section C on *page twenty-eight*

DO NOT WRITE IN THIS MARGIN

SECTION C

Marks

Both questions in this section should be attempted.

Note that each question contains a choice.

Questions 1 and 2 should be attempted on the blank pages which follow.
All answers must be written clearly and legibly in ink.

Supplementary sheets, if required, may be obtained from the invigilator.

1. Answer **either** A **or** B.

A. The diagrams below show the two stages of photosynthesis.

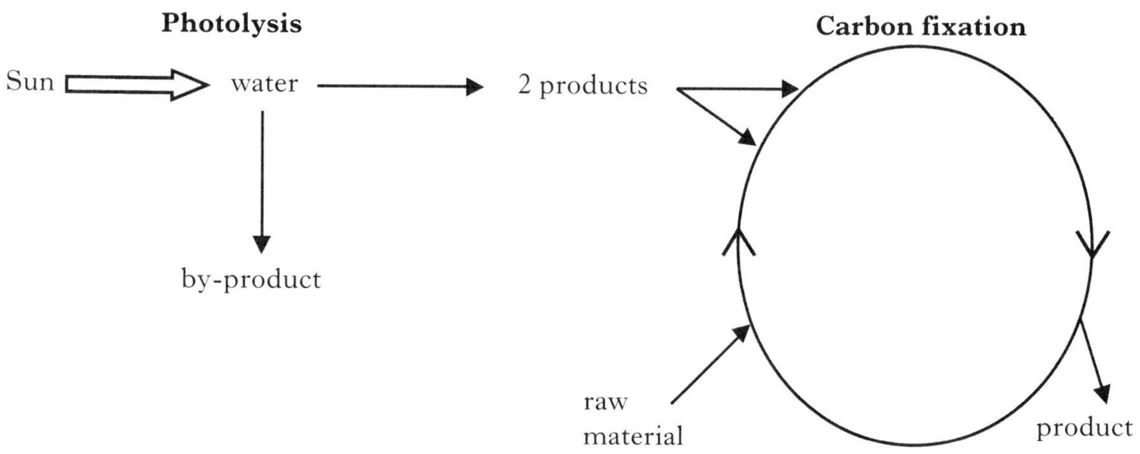

Describe what happens during the two stages

(*a*) photolysis

and

(*b*) carbon fixation. **5**

OR

B. The diagrams below show animal and plant cells in isotonic solutions.
These diagrams are not to scale.

Animal cells

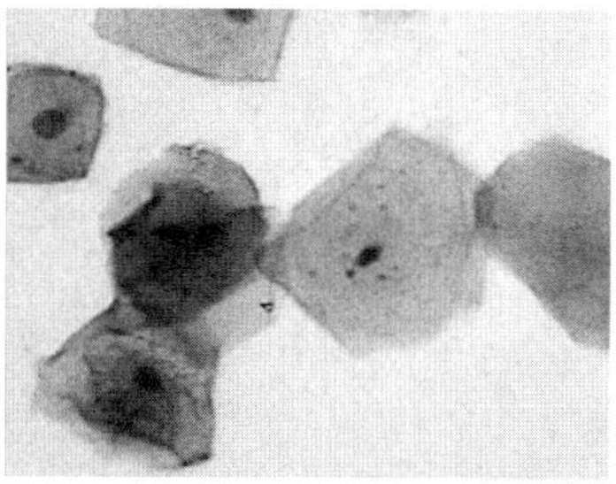

Plant cells

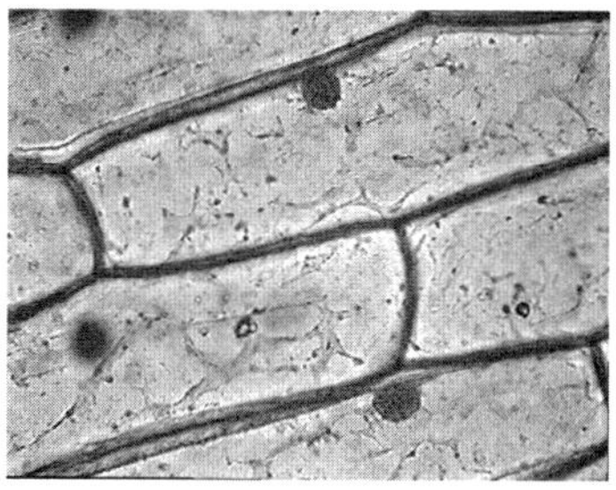

Describe the osmotic effect of transferring

(*a*) the animal cells into a hypotonic solution (water)

(*b*) the plant cells into a hypertonic solution (strong salt). **5**

Question 2 is on *Page thirty*

DO NOT WRITE IN THIS MARGIN

SPACE FOR ANSWER TO QUESTION 1

[Turn over for Question 2 on *Page thirty*

DO NOT WRITE IN THIS MARGIN

Marks

2. Answer **either** A **or** B.

Labelled diagrams may be included where appropriate.

A. Describe the role of the liver and pancreas in digestion. Include in your answer the processing of absorbed materials such as glucose and amino acids. **5**

OR

B. Describe the role of antibodies and phagocytosis in defence. Name the cells involved in each of these defence mechanisms. **5**

[*END OF QUESTION PAPER*]

DO NOT WRITE IN THIS MARGIN

SPACE FOR ANSWER TO QUESTION 2

DO NOT WRITE IN THIS MARGIN

ADDITIONAL SPACE FOR ANSWERS

ADDITIONAL GRAPH PAPER FOR QUESTION 2(*d*)

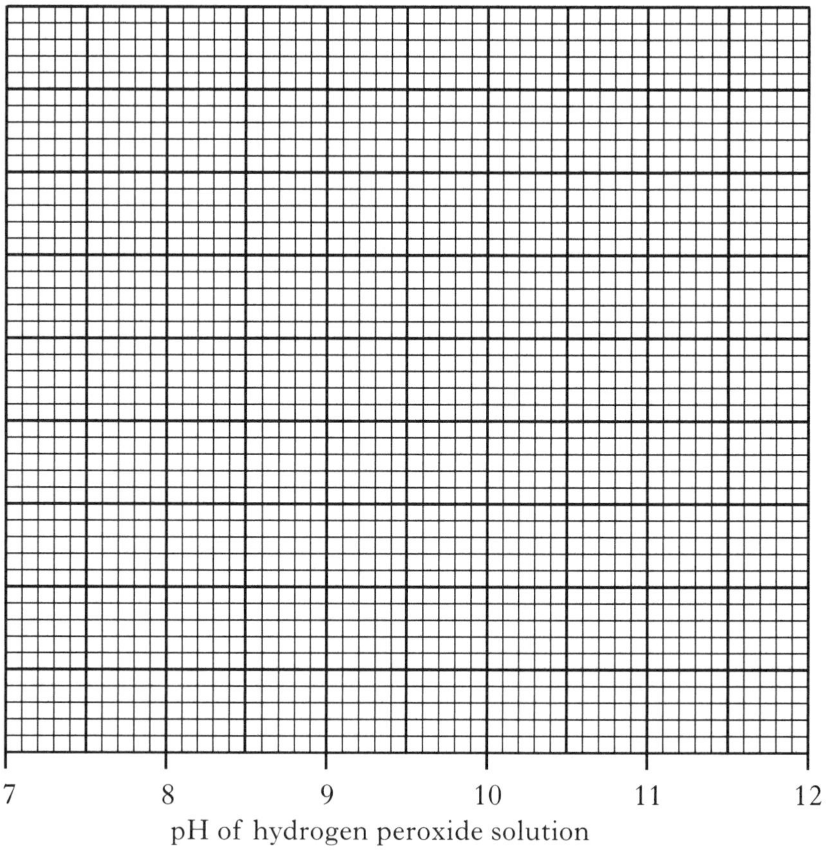

DO NOT WRITE IN THIS MARGIN

ADDITIONAL SPACE FOR ANSWERS

DO NOT WRITE IN THIS MARGIN

ADDITIONAL SPACE FOR ANSWERS

INTERMEDIATE 2
2010

[BLANK PAGE]

FOR OFFICIAL USE

Total for Sections B and C

X007/201

NATIONAL QUALIFICATIONS 2010

THURSDAY, 27 MAY
9.00 AM – 11.00 AM

BIOLOGY INTERMEDIATE 2

Fill in these boxes and read what is printed below.

Full name of centre

Town

Forename(s)

Surname

Date of birth

Day Month Year

Scottish candidate number

Number of seat

SECTION A (25 marks)

Instructions for completion of Section A are given on page two.

For this section of the examination you must use an HB pencil.

SECTIONS B AND C (75 marks)

1 (a) All questions should be attempted.

(b) It should be noted that in **Section C** questions 1 and 2 each contain a choice.

2 The questions may be answered in any order but all answers are to be written in the spaces provided in this answer book, **and must be written clearly and legibly in ink**.

3 Additional space for answers will be found at the end of the book. If further space is required, supplementary sheets may be obtained from the Invigilator and should be inserted inside the **front** cover of this book.

4 The numbers of questions must be clearly inserted with any answers written in the additional space.

5 Rough work, if any should be necessary, should be written in this book and then scored through when the fair copy has been written. If further space is required, a supplementary sheet for rough work may be obtained from the Invigilator.

6 Before leaving the examination room you must give this book to the Invigilator. If you do not, you may lose all the marks for this paper.

Read carefully

1 Check that the answer sheet provided is for **Biology Intermediate 2 (Section A)**.

2 For this section of the examination you must use an **HB pencil** and, where necessary, an eraser.

3 Check that the answer sheet you have been given has **your name**, **date of birth**, **SCN** (Scottish Candidate Number) and **Centre Name** printed on it.

Do not change any of these details.

4 If any of this information is wrong, tell the Invigilator immediately.

5 If this information is correct, **print** your name and seat number in the boxes provided.

6 The answer to each question is **either** A, B, C or D. Decide what your answer is, then, using your pencil, put a horizontal line in the space provided (see sample question below).

7 There is **only one correct** answer to each question.

8 Any rough working should be done on the question paper or the rough working sheet, **not** on your answer sheet.

9 At the end of the exam, put the **answer sheet for Section A inside the front cover of this answer book**.

Sample Question

Plants compete mainly for

A water, light and soil nutrients

B water, food and soil nutrients

C light, water and food

D light, food and soil nutrients.

The correct answer is **A**—water, light and soil nutrients. The answer **A** has been clearly marked in **pencil** with a horizontal line (see below).

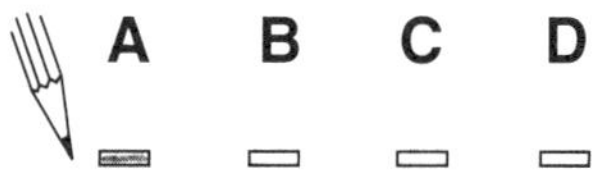

Changing an answer

If you decide to change your answer, carefully erase your first answer and using your pencil, fill in the answer you want. The answer below has been changed to **D**.

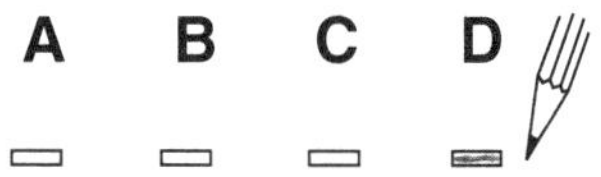

SECTION A

All questions in this Section should be attempted.

1. Four thin sections of onion tissue were immersed in 5% sugar solution.

The sections were left for 15 minutes then viewed under a microscope.

The table below shows the percentage of cells plasmolysed in each section.

Section	*Cells plasmolysed* (%)
1	44
2	44
3	54
4	58

The average percentage of cells plasmolysed is

A 44

B 50

C 54

D 200.

2. The diagram below shows the initial diameter of a potato disc.

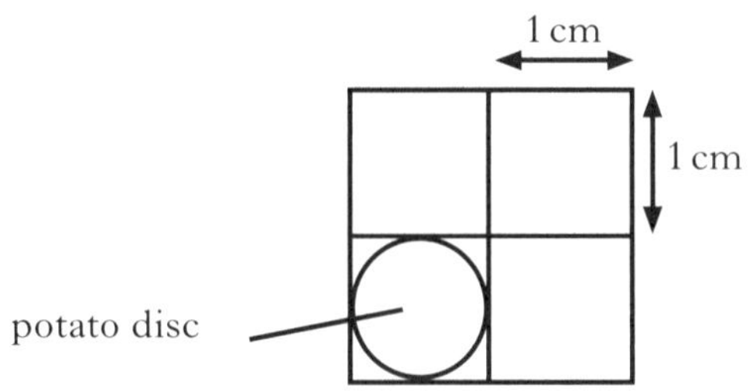

The potato disc was placed in a hypotonic solution for one hour.

Which of the following diagrams shows correctly the change in the diameter of the potato disc?

A

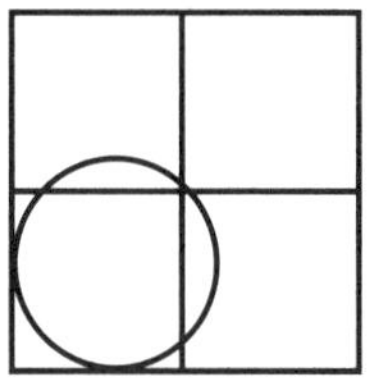

B

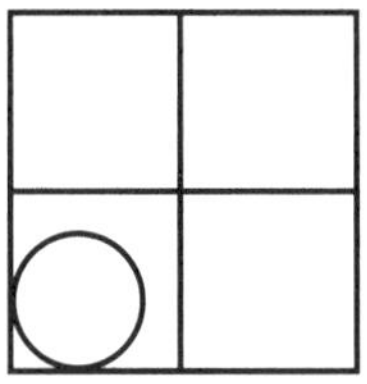

C

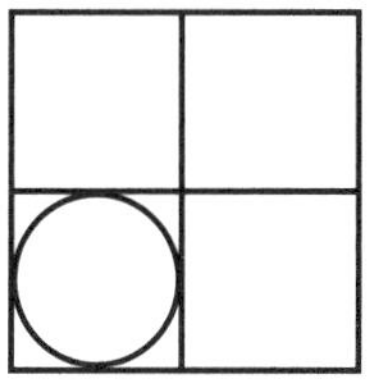

D

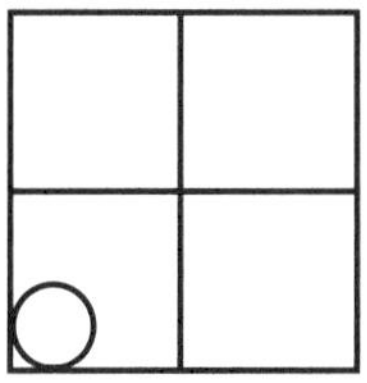

3. One of the properties of enzymes in the initiation of chemical reactions is that an enzyme

A does not alter the energy input required

B raises the energy input required

C lowers the energy input required

D raises then lowers the energy input required.

4. Which term refers to the process by which complex molecules are formed from simple molecules?

A Digestion

B Synthesis

C Degradation

D Respiration

5. Which of the following correctly describes amylase?

A It breaks down starch into amino acids.

B It builds up glucose-1-phosphate into starch.

C It breaks down proteins into peptides.

D It breaks down starch into maltose.

6. A plant cell, which was placed in a liquid, gained water by osmosis.

When compared to the liquid, the cell contents are described as being

A plasmolysed

B hypertonic

C hypotonic

D flaccid.

7. Which of the following increases in the muscles of an athlete and causes muscle fatigue during a race?

A Lactic acid

B Glucose

C Oxygen

D ATP

8. The following experiment was set up.

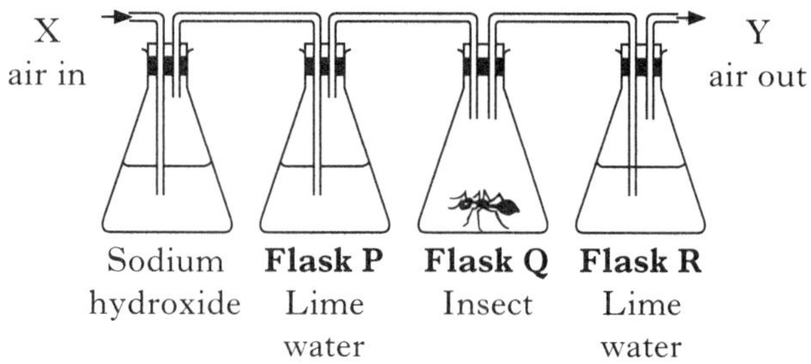

Sodium hydroxide solution absorbs carbon dioxide from air.

Lime water turns from clear to cloudy in the presence of carbon dioxide.

Air is drawn through the apparatus from X to Y, passing through each flask in turn.

Predict what would happen to the results if two insects were used in flask Q. The lime water in

A Flask P turns cloudy more slowly

B Flask P turns cloudy more quickly

C Flask R turns cloudy more slowly

D Flask R turns cloudy more quickly.

9. The diagrams below show four experiments used to investigate the conditions needed for photosynthesis.

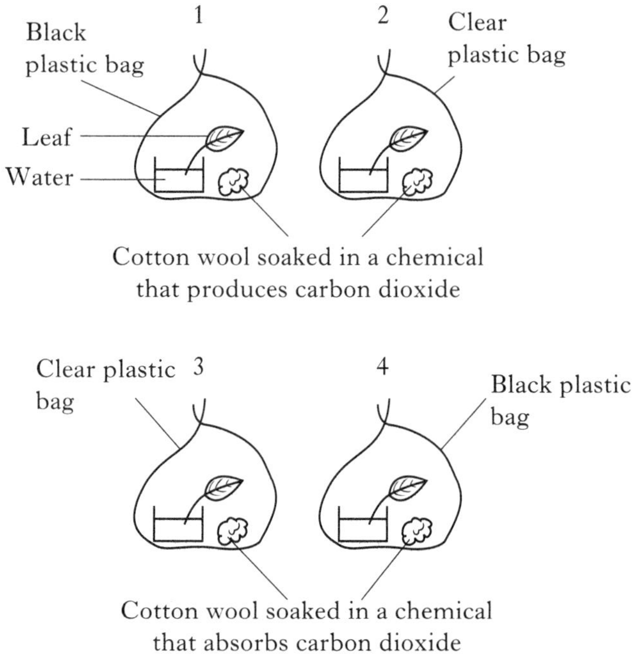

After two days, the four leaves were tested for the presence of starch.

The results from which two experiments should be compared to show that carbon dioxide is needed for photosynthesis?

A 1 and 2

B 2 and 4

C 2 and 3

D 3 and 4

10. A species can be defined as a group of organisms which

A breed together to produce fertile offspring

B have the same phenotypes

C contain the same number of chromosomes

D contain identical genetic material.

11. The graph below shows the average number of peppered moths, in a woodland, in June of each year over a 10 year period.

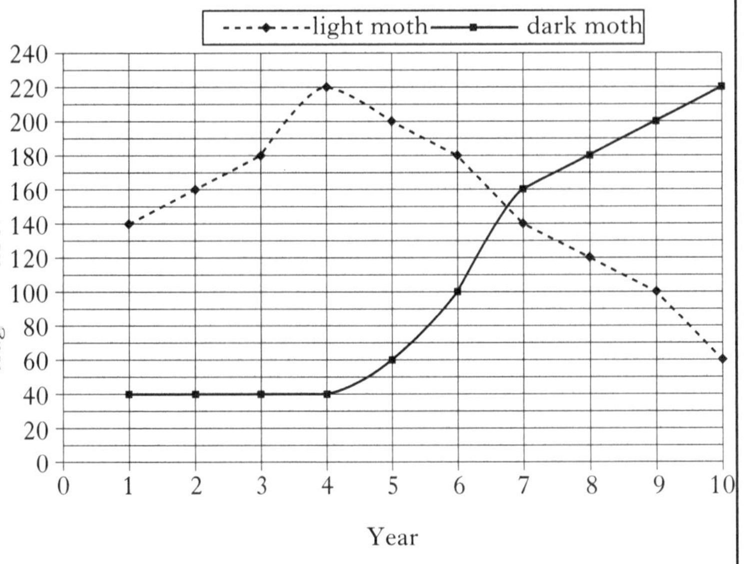

Studies have shown that an increase in the number of dark moths is related to an increase in the level of pollution in the atmosphere.

Which of the following best describes what would happen to the number of moths if measures were introduced to reduce air pollution in year 10?

	Light moth	*Dark moth*
A	decrease	increase
B	increase	decrease
C	increase	increase
D	decrease	decrease

12. The diagram below shows the main parts of a flower.

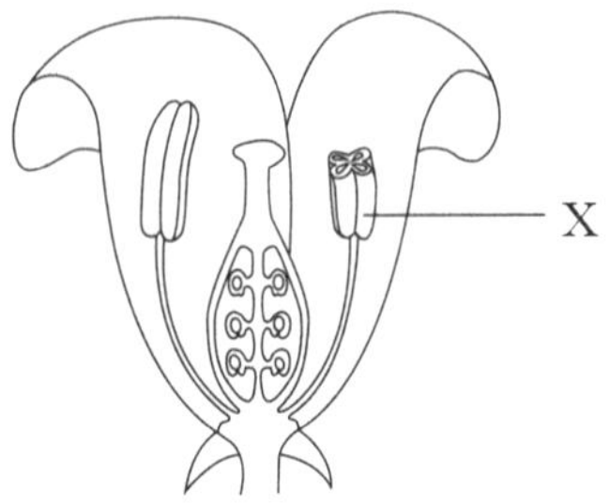

Which line in the table identifies X and the type of gamete it produces?

	Name of X	*Type of gamete produced*
A	ovary	male
B	ovary	female
C	anther	female
D	anther	male

13. The diagram below shows a stage in the process of reproduction.

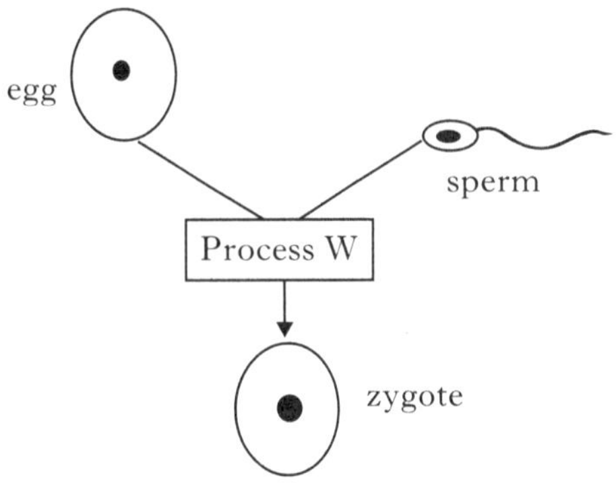

Process W is

A meiosis

B fertilisation

C gamete production

D random assortment.

[Turn over

14. Sperm production in humans is controlled by two hormones, P and Q.

As levels of P rise, sperm production increases.

As levels of Q rise, sperm production decreases.

Which of the graphs below shows the changes in hormone levels of a man whose sperm production is decreasing?

A
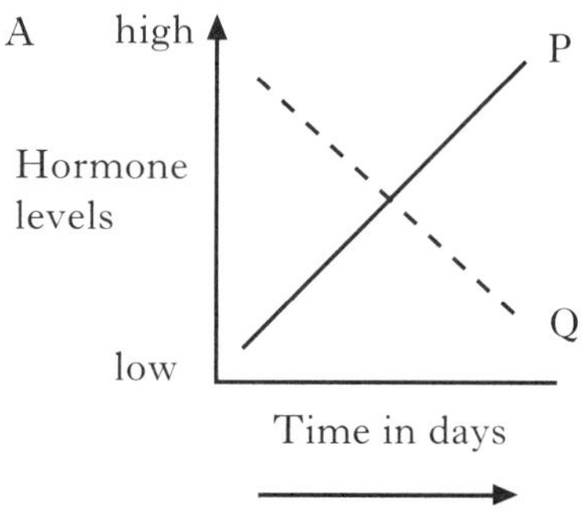

B
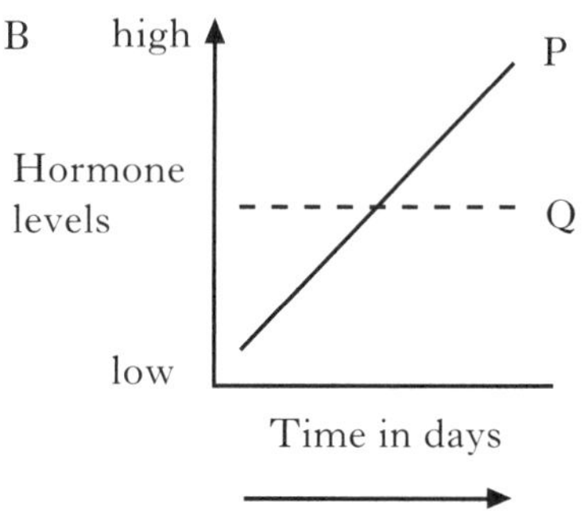

C
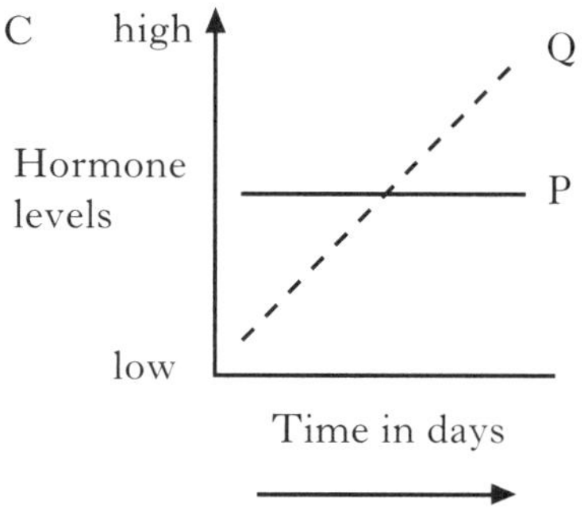

D
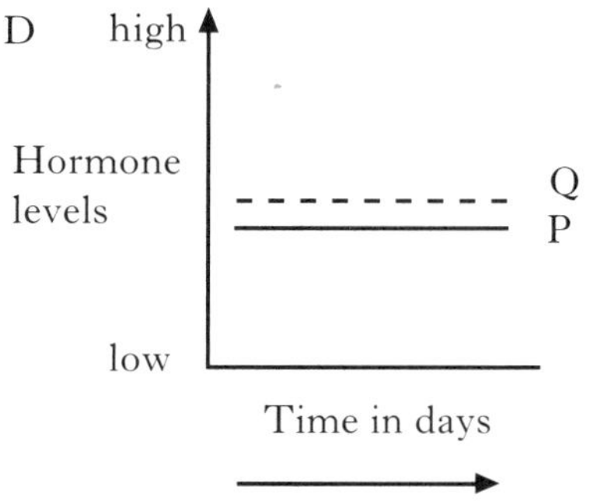

15. DNA determines the structure and function of a type of molecule in the cell. The molecule is

A protein

B fat

C amino acid

D carbohydrate.

16. In humans, the allele for blood group A is dominant to the allele for blood group O.

Two parents both have blood group A. Their child has blood group O.

What is the best explanation for this pattern of inheritance?

A The child has inherited the blood group directly from a grandparent.

B The parents are homozygous for the blood group alleles.

C The parents are heterozygous for the blood group alleles.

D There has been a mutation in the blood group alleles.

17. Which line in the table below identifies correctly one advantage and one disadvantage of genetic engineering to make desired products?

	Advantage	*Disadvantage*
A	increased rate of production	cost of development
B	cost of development	possible release of genetically engineered bacteria into the environment
C	increased range of products	increased rate of production
D	increased rate of production	increased range of products

18. The table below shows the composition of a 200 cm^3 serving of low fat milk.

Composition	*200 cm^3 low fat milk provides*
protein	6·0 g
carbohydrate	10·0 g
fat	0·2 g

What is the simplest whole number ratio of the mass of protein to carbohydrate to fat?

A 3 : 5 : 0·1

B 6 : 10 : 0·2

C 30 : 50 : 1

D 60 : 100 : 2

19. The table below shows the composition of inhaled air and exhaled air.

	Inhaled air (%)	*Exhaled air* (%)
Oxygen	20	16
Carbon dioxide	0·04	4

How many times greater is the oxygen concentration in inhaled air than in exhaled air?

A 0·08

B 1·25

C 4

D 320

20. The list below refers to features of a capillary network.

1 It has a large surface area.

2 It is in close contact with tissue cells.

3 Capillaries are thin walled.

Which statements refer to features that allow efficient gas exchange?

A 1 and 2 only

B 1 and 3 only

C 2 and 3 only

D 1, 2 and 3

21. The graph below shows the relationship between oxygen concentration and the concentration of oxyhaemoglobin.

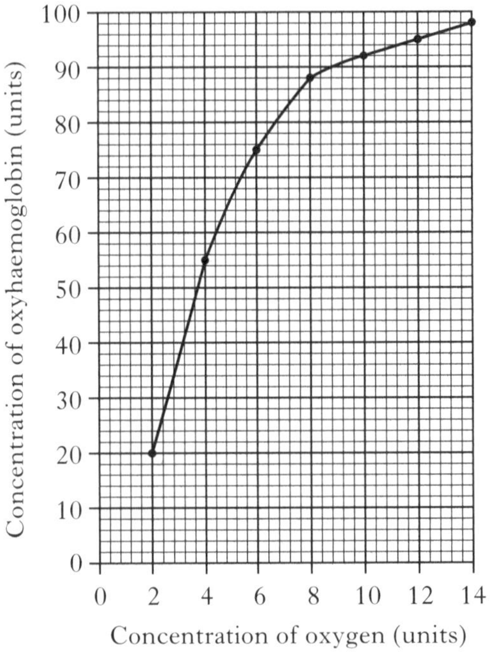

What is the percentage increase in the concentration of oxyhaemoglobin when the concentration of oxygen increases from 2 units to 4 units?

A 2

B 35

C 55

D 175

22. Which of the following produce antibodies?

A Blood plasma

B Lymphocytes

C Macrophages

D Red blood cells

[Turn over

23. The diagram below shows a human brain.

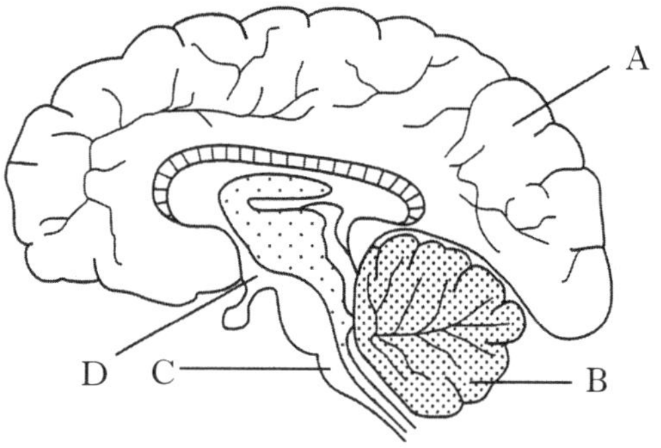

Which letter shows the site that controls heart rate and breathing rate?

24. The following stages occur in a reflex action.

1 The effector produces a response.

2 A sense organ is stimulated.

3 An impulse passes along a sensory neurone.

4 An impulse passes along a motor neurone.

The correct order of the stages is

A 2, 3, 4, 1

B 2, 1, 4, 3

C 1, 2, 3, 4

D 3, 4, 1, 2.

25. Which of the following pathways shows the correct response by blood vessels in the skin to a decrease in body temperature?

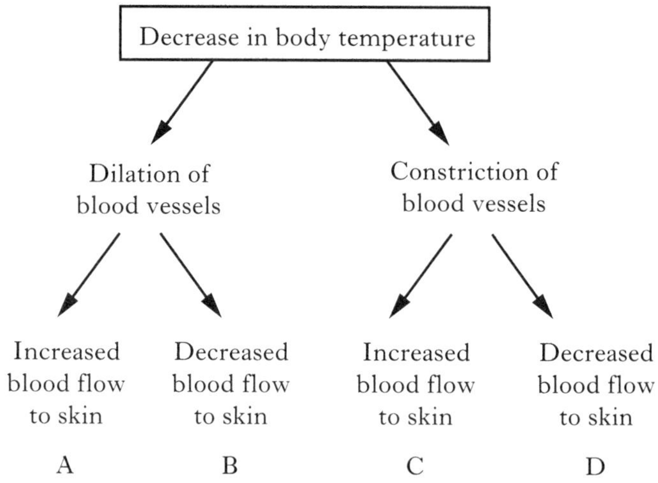

Candidates are reminded that the answer sheet for Section A MUST be placed INSIDE the front cover of this answer book.

[Turn over for Section B on *Page ten*

DO NOT WRITE IN THIS MARGIN

Marks

SECTION B

All questions in this section should be attempted.
All answers must be written clearly and legibly in ink.

1. (*a*) The diagram below shows two cells P and Q.

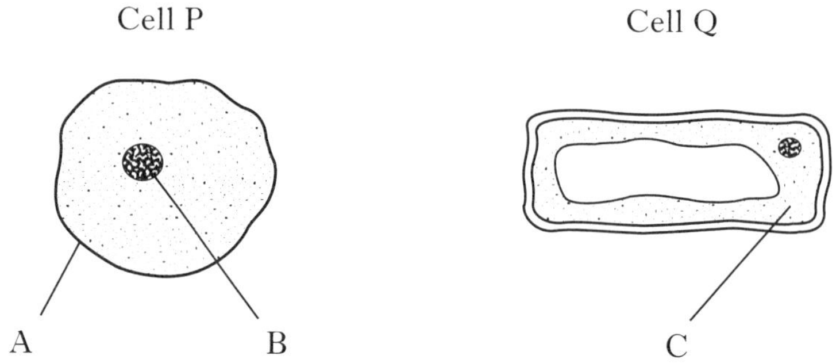

(i) Complete the table below to give the name and function of the parts labelled A, B and C.

Letter	*Part*	*Function*
A	cell membrane	
B	nucleus	
C		site of cell activities

2

(ii) Which cell is a plant cell? Give a reason for your choice.

Cell ________________

Reason ____ **1**

(*b*) Cells have commercial and industrial uses.

(i) One type of cell is used in the production of yoghurt.

(A) Name the type of cell used in the production of yoghurt.

________________________ **1**

(B) Name the milk sugar used by these cells.

________________________ **1**

DO NOT WRITE IN THIS MARGIN

Marks

1. **(*b*) (continued)**

(ii) Underline **one** option in each set of brackets to make the following sentence correct.

Gasohol is produced when cells act on sugar to produce { alcohol / methane }

which is then mixed with { ethanol / petrol }. **1**

(iii) Fungal cells are used to produce antibiotics. What is the function of antibiotics in the treatment of disease?

____ **1**

[Turn over

DO NOT WRITE IN THIS MARGIN

Marks

2. (*a*) Liver contains the enzyme catalase. A piece of liver was added to hydrogen peroxide and foam was produced as shown below.

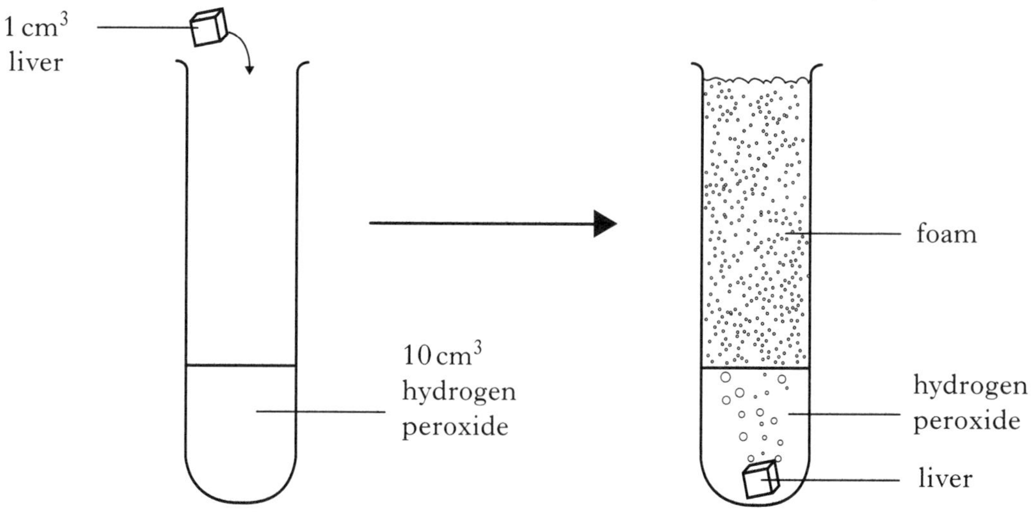

(i) Name the gas in the foam.

______________________________ **1**

(ii) Which other product was formed during this reaction?

______________________________ **1**

(iii) Describe a control which would be used to show that active catalase is needed for this experiment.

____

______________________________ **1**

(iv) How could the activity of catalase be measured in this experiment?

____

______________________________ **1**

DO NOT WRITE IN THIS MARGIN

Marks

2. **(continued)**

(*b*) The diagram below shows an investigation to compare the activity of catalase in apple and liver.

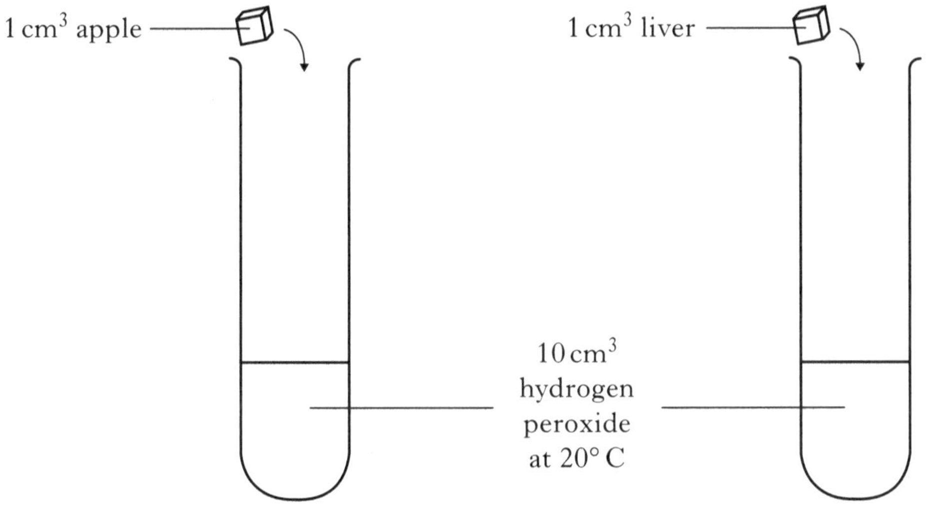

State **two** variables, not shown in the diagram, that must be kept constant for a valid comparison.

1 ______________________________

2 ______________________________ **2**

(*c*) Explain why enzyme activity decreases at temperatures above the optimum.

____

______________________________ **1**

[Turn over

DO NOT WRITE IN THIS MARGIN

Marks

3. (*a*) Cells need ATP for cell division. ATP is produced during the aerobic respiration of glucose.

How many ATP molecules are produced per glucose molecule in this process?

____________________ **1**

(*b*) The diagram below shows dividing root cells which carry out aerobic respiration.

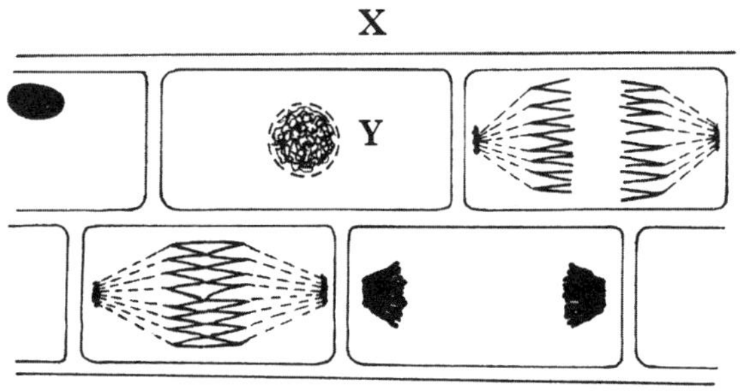

Carbon dioxide is one waste product of aerobic respiration.

Tick (✓) the appropriate box below to show the direction of diffusion of carbon dioxide.

X ⟶ Y ☐

Y ⟶ X ☐ **1**

(*c*) Aerobic respiration occurs in two stages. Name the first stage of aerobic respiration and a product, other than ATP.

Name ________________________ **1**

Product ________________________ **1**

DO NOT WRITE IN THIS MARGIN

Marks

4. The graph below shows the effects of two different environmental factors on the rate of photosynthesis.

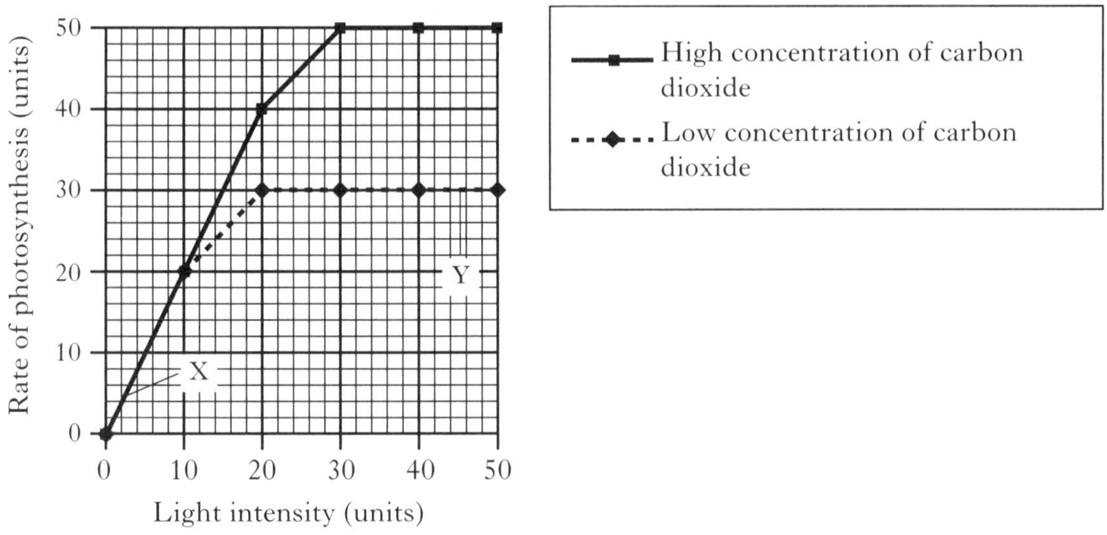

(*a*) What are the limiting factors at points X and Y?

X ______________________________ **1**

Y ______________________________ **1**

(*b*) Suggest **one** way that the rate of photosynthesis can be measured.

____

______________________________ **1**

(*c*) During the first stage of photosynthesis, light energy is used.

(i) Where is light energy trapped in the cell?

______________________________ **1**

(ii) State **one** use of this light energy.

______________________________ **1**

(*d*) (i) Name the second stage of photosynthesis.

______________________________ **1**

(ii) Name the carbohydrate produced during the second stage of photosynthesis.

______________________________ **1**

DO NOT WRITE IN THIS MARGIN

Marks

5. The diagram below shows part of an Antarctic food web.

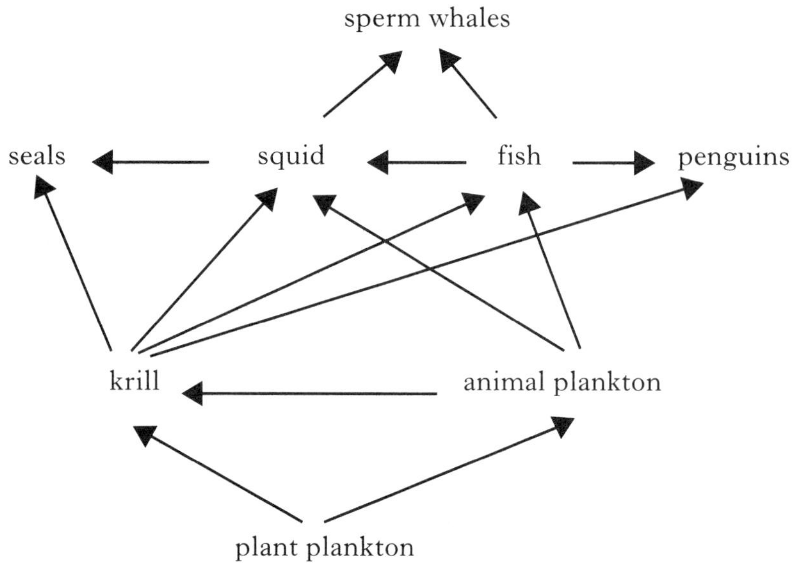

(*a*) Explain why a decrease in sperm whale numbers may lead to an increase in seal numbers.

____

____ **1**

(*b*) Decide if each of the following statements is **True** or **False**, and tick (✓) the appropriate box.

If the statement is **False**, write the correct word in the **Correction box** to replace the word(s) underlined in the statement.

Statement	*True*	*False*	*Correction*
In this food web, krill are <u>herbivores</u>.			
The population of <u>sperm whales</u> has the highest biomass.			
The range of species in a <u>population</u> is called biodiversity.			

3

DO NOT WRITE IN THIS MARGIN

Marks

6. (*a*) In shorthorn cattle, the allele for red coat colour (R) is co-dominant with the allele for white coat colour (W). Heterozygous shorthorn cattle have a mixture of red and white hairs and are described as "roan".

(i) State the genotype of white cattle.

______________________ **1**

(ii) A red female and roan male were crossed. Complete the Punnett square below to show the expected results of this cross.

		Genotype of gametes of roan male	
Genotype of gametes of red female	R		
	R		

2

(*b*) Seed mass in plants is controlled by several genes. Name this type of inheritance.

______________________________________ **1**

(*c*) Decide if each of the following human characteristics shows **continuous** or **discontinuous** variation. Tick (✓) the appropriate boxes.

Human characteristic	*Type of variation*	
	continuous	*discontinuous*
Blood group		
Height		

1

(*d*) As an organism grows and develops, it is affected by environmental impact. What is the meaning of the term environmental impact?

____

______________________________________ **1**

DO NOT WRITE IN THIS MARGIN

Marks

7. Four groups of students investigated the effect of light intensity on the time taken for larvae to travel 10 cm. The light intensity was varied by moving the light source. The diagram below shows the apparatus.

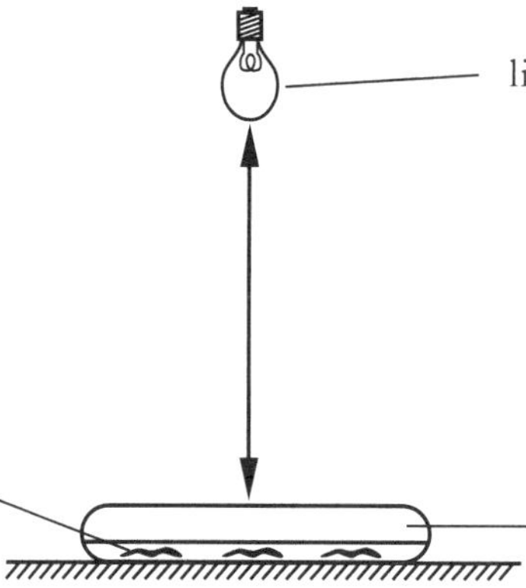

The table below shows the results of this investigation.

Light intensity	*Time taken for larvae to travel 10 cm* (s)				
	Group 1	*Group 2*	*Group 3*	*Group 4*	*Average*
High	20	22	24	22	22
Medium	39	42	47	44	43
Low	48	50	50	52	50
Very low	66	70	64	76	

(*a*) Complete the table to show the average time taken to travel 10 cm in very low light intensity. **1**

Space for calculation

(*b*) Which light intensity showed the greatest **range** of results?

____________________________ **1**

DO NOT WRITE IN THIS MARGIN

Marks

7. (continued)

(*c*) On the grid below, plot a **bar graph** to show the **average** time taken for larvae to travel 10 cm in high, medium and low light intensity levels **only**.

(Additional graph paper, if required, will be found on *Page thirty*.)

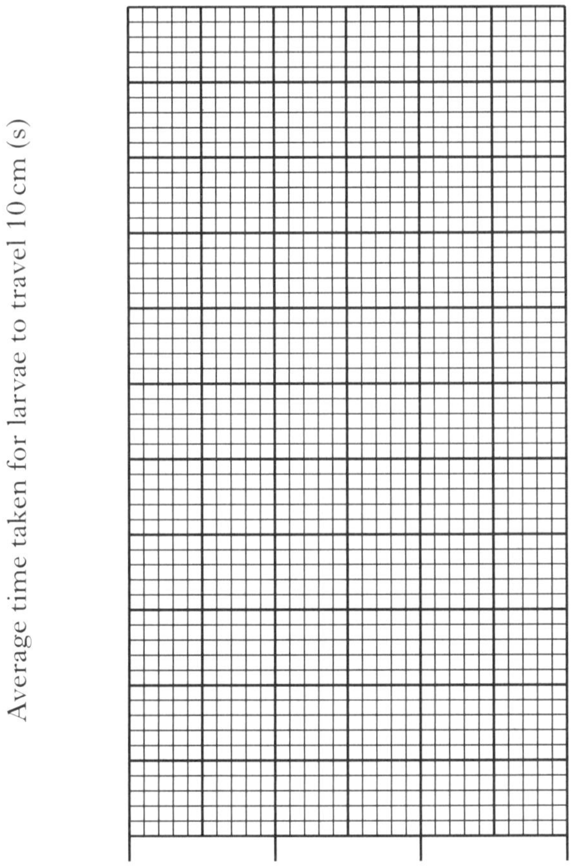

3

(*d*) Describe the relationship between light intensity and time taken for larvae to travel 10 cm.

____

____ 1

[Turn over

DO NOT WRITE IN THIS MARGIN

Marks

8. Swans and cygnets (young swans) live on the River Ayr. Foxes in the area kill and eat cygnets.

(*a*) (i) Underline **one** option in each set of brackets to make the following sentences correct.

Cygnets are the { predators / prey } of foxes.

The foxes are { primary / secondary } consumers. **1**

(ii) Fifty cygnets were counted in 2008. By 2009, 18 of these cygnets had been killed by foxes. What percentage of the cygnets survived to 2009?

Space for calculation

__________ % **1**

(*b*) Dead adult swans were found throughout the year. It was discovered that the use of lead weights by anglers was poisoning the swans. Other animals in the river were also affected by the lead.

Suggest the effect of the lead on the biodiversity of a river ecosystem.

Explain your answer.

Effect ______________________________

Explanation ____

____ **1**

(*c*) State another type of pollution which may affect biodiversity in the river.

____ **1**

DO NOT WRITE IN THIS MARGIN

Marks

9. The diagram below shows the human digestive system.

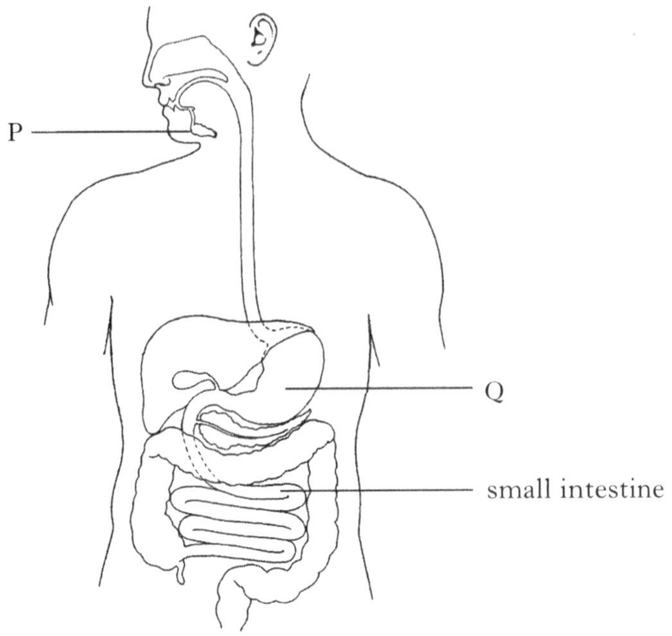

(*a*) Name the digestive enzymes produced by P and Q.

P ______________________ 1

Q ______________________ 1

(*b*) Describe how the action of peristalsis moves food through the small intestine.

____

____

____ 2

(*c*) Give **two** features of the small intestine which increases the rate of absorption.

1 ____ 1

2 ____ 1

[Turn over

DO NOT WRITE IN THIS MARGIN

Marks

10. The diagram below represents the human circulatory system.

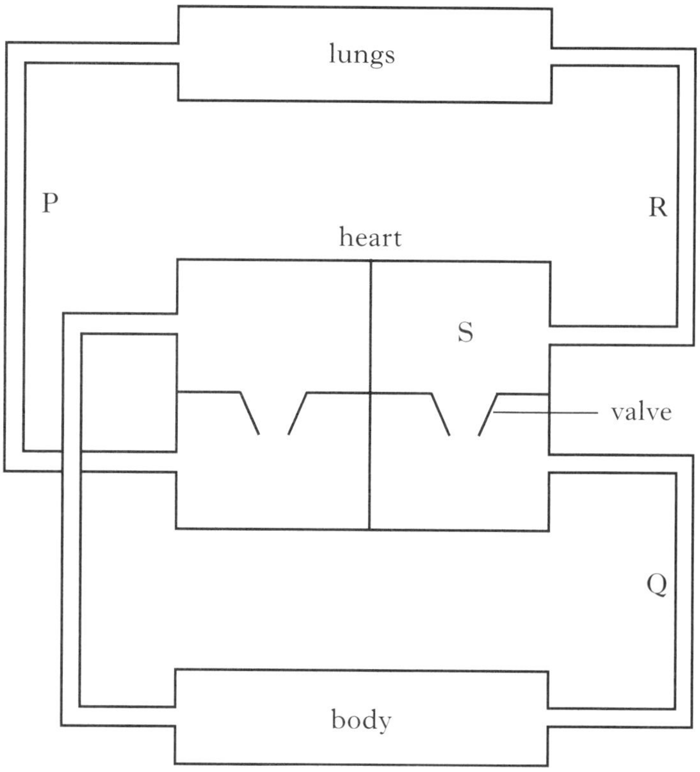

(*a*) (i) Draw arrows at P and Q to show the direction of blood flow in these vessels. **1**

(ii) State whether the blood is oxygenated or deoxygenated in vessels P and Q.

P ______________________

Q ______________________ **1**

(*b*) Name heart chamber S and blood vessel R.

Heart chamber S ______________________ **1**

Blood vessel R ______________________ **1**

(*c*) What is the function of the heart valves?

______________________ **1**

(*d*) Explain why a blocked coronary artery damages heart muscle.

____

______________________ **1**

DO NOT WRITE IN THIS MARGIN

Marks

11. The following diagram represents a kidney nephron.

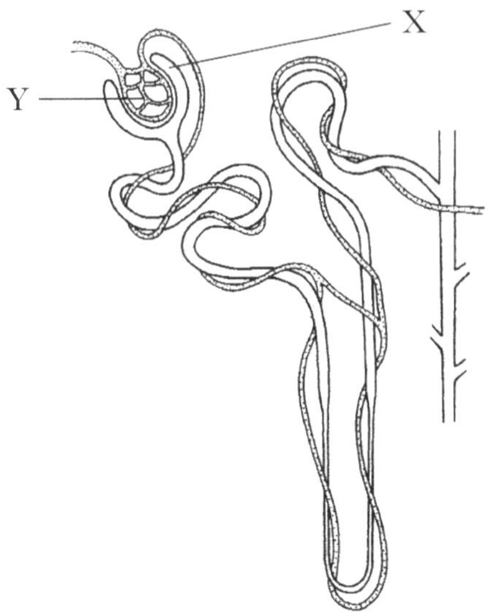

(*a*) The following sentences describe some processes that occur in the nephron.

Underline **one** option in each set of brackets to make the sentences correct.

The glomerulus is shown by letter { X / Y } and the process carried out in this structure is { absorption / filtration }.

An increase in the hormone ADH causes { less / more } water to be taken back into the blood. **2**

(*b*) Urea is the nitrogenous waste product removed in the urine.

Where is urea produced?

____________________ **1**

(*c*) What term is used for the control of water content in organisms?

____ **1**

[Turn over

DO NOT WRITE IN THIS MARGIN

Marks

12. A scientist measured the reaction times of five students before and after drinking alcohol.

Average reaction times were calculated for each student.

The graph below shows their average reaction times before and after drinking alcohol.

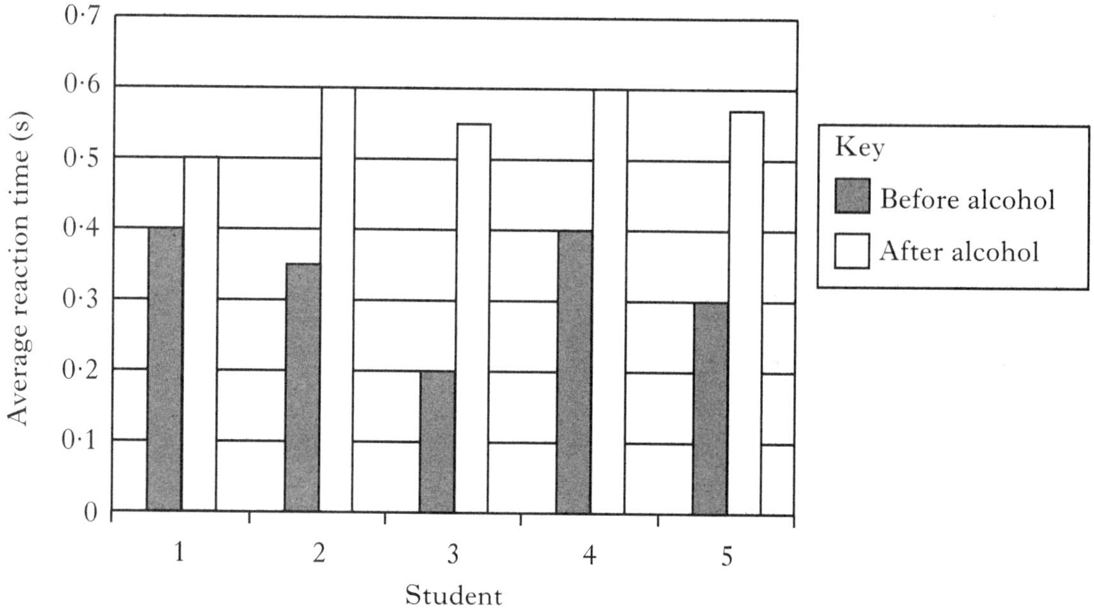

(*a*) What conclusion can be drawn from the results?

____

____ **1**

(*b*) Why did the scientist calculate the **average** reaction times?

____

____ **1**

(*c*) What is the percentage increase in the average reaction time for student 4 after drinking alcohol?

Space for calculation

______________ % **1**

(*d*) In this investigation, the students had to press a switch when a light flashed.

Which part of the brain coordinates this movement?

____ **1**

[Turn over for Section C on *Page twenty-six*

Marks

SECTION C

Both questions in this section should be attempted.

Note that each question contains a choice.

Questions 1 and 2 should be attempted on the blank pages which follow. All answers must be written clearly and legibly in ink.

Supplementary sheets, if required, may be obtained from the Invigilator.

1. Answer **either** A **or** B.

A. The diagrams below show structures which are involved in the transport of oxygen.

Lungs

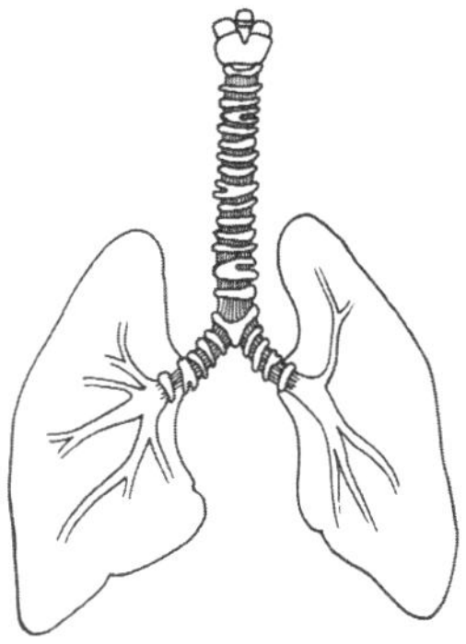

Air sac

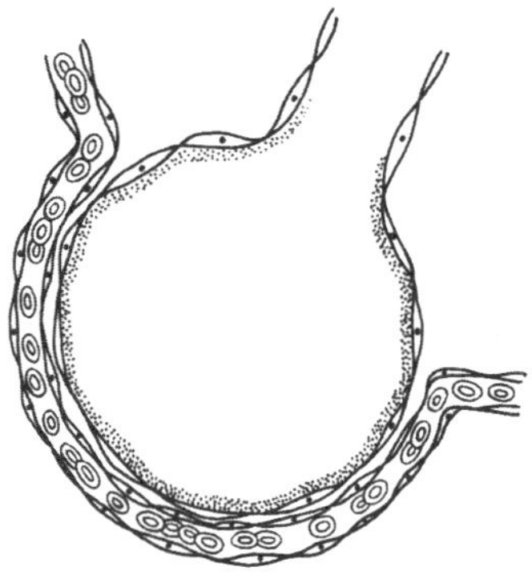

Capillary bed in the skin

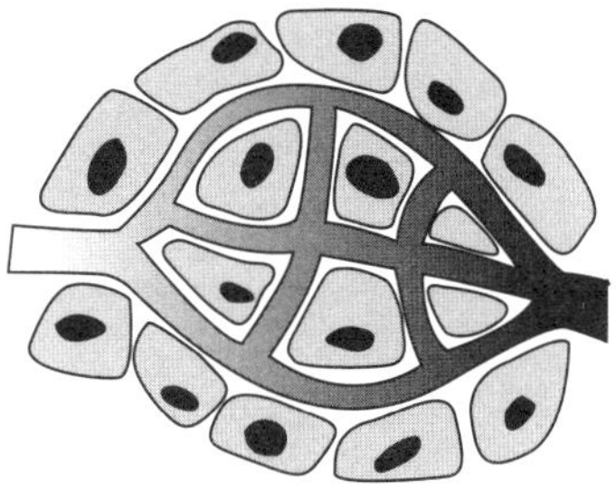

Describe the path taken by oxygen through these structures from the air to a skin cell. **5**

OR

B. The diagrams below represent the complex molecules of the three main food groups.

Carbohydrate

Fat

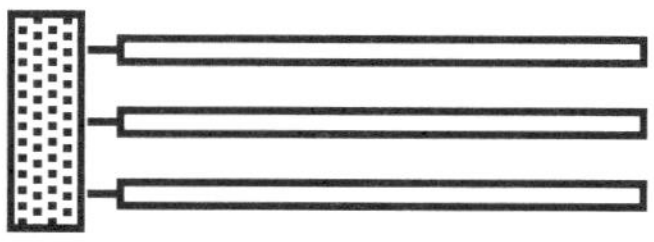

Protein

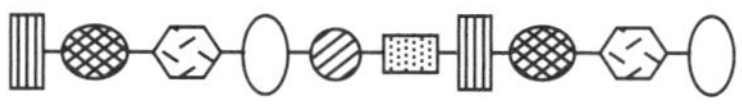

Give a role of each food group and describe these three molecules in terms of their chemical elements and simple structures. **5**

Question 2 is on *Page twenty-eight*.

DO NOT WRITE IN THIS MARGIN

SPACE FOR ANSWER TO QUESTION 1

[Turn over for Question 2 on *Page twenty-eight*

Marks

2. Answer **either** A **or** B.

Labelled diagrams may be included where appropriate.

A. Describe **three** structural adaptations of desert plants and explain how these adaptations increase their chances of survival. **5**

OR

B. Describe the differences between the chromosomes in human body cells and human gametes. Explain how these chromosomes are involved in sex determination. **5**

[*END OF QUESTION PAPER*]

DO NOT WRITE IN THIS MARGIN

SPACE FOR ANSWER TO QUESTION 2

DO NOT WRITE IN THIS MARGIN

ADDITIONAL SPACE FOR ANSWERS

ADDITIONAL GRAPH PAPER FOR QUESTION 7(*c*)

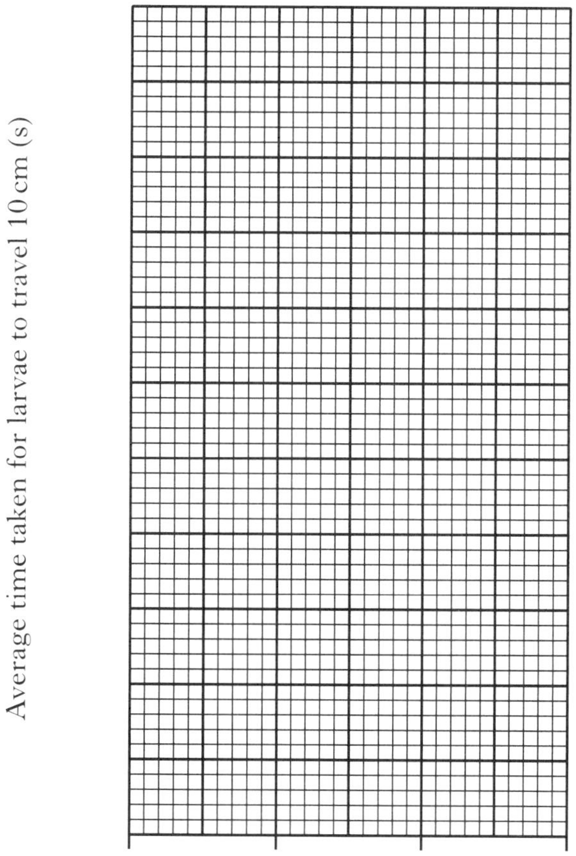

INTERMEDIATE 2

2011

[BLANK PAGE]

FOR OFFICIAL USE

Total for Sections B and C

X007/201

NATIONAL QUALIFICATIONS 2011

WEDNESDAY, 1 JUNE 9.00 AM – 11.00 AM

BIOLOGY INTERMEDIATE 2

Fill in these boxes and read what is printed below.

Full name of centre

Town

Forename(s)

Surname

Date of birth

Day Month Year

Scottish candidate number

Number of seat

SECTION A (25 marks)

Instructions for completion of Section A are given on page two.

For this section of the examination you must use an HB pencil.

SECTIONS B AND C (75 marks)

1 (a) All questions should be attempted.

(b) It should be noted that in **Section C** questions 1 and 2 each contain a choice.

2 The questions may be answered in any order but all answers are to be written in the spaces provided in this answer book, **and must be written clearly and legibly in ink**.

3 Additional space for answers will be found at the end of the book. If further space is required, supplementary sheets may be obtained from the Invigilator and should be inserted inside the **front** cover of this book.

4 The numbers of questions must be clearly inserted with any answers written in the additional space.

5 Rough work, if any should be necessary, should be written in this book and then scored through when the fair copy has been written. If further space is required, a supplementary sheet for rough work may be obtained from the Invigilator.

6 Before leaving the examination room you must give this book to the Invigilator. If you do not, you may lose all the marks for this paper.

Read carefully

1 Check that the answer sheet provided is for **Biology Intermediate 2 (Section A)**.

2 For this section of the examination you must use an **HB pencil** and, where necessary, an eraser.

3 Check that the answer sheet you have been given has **your name**, **date of birth**, **SCN** (Scottish Candidate Number) and **Centre Name** printed on it.

Do not change any of these details.

4 If any of this information is wrong, tell the Invigilator immediately.

5 If this information is correct, **print** your name and seat number in the boxes provided.

6 The answer to each question is **either** A, B, C or D. Decide what your answer is, then, using your pencil, put a horizontal line in the space provided (see sample question below).

7 There is **only one correct** answer to each question.

8 Any rough working should be done on the question paper or the rough working sheet, **not** on your answer sheet.

9 At the end of the exam, put the **answer sheet for Section A inside the front cover of this answer book**.

Sample Question

Plants compete mainly for

A water, light and soil nutrients

B water, food and soil nutrients

C light, water and food

D light, food and soil nutrients.

The correct answer is **A**—water, light and soil nutrients. The answer **A** has been clearly marked in **pencil** with a horizontal line (see below).

Changing an answer

If you decide to change your answer, carefully erase your first answer and using your pencil, fill in the answer you want. The answer below has been changed to **D**.

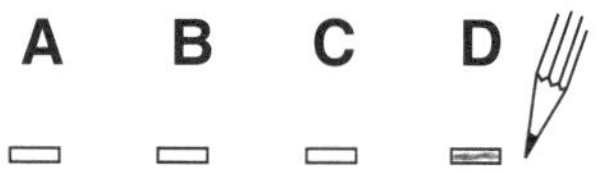

SECTION A

All questions in this Section should be attempted.

1. Which substance enters animal cells by diffusion and is used to produce ATP?

A Carbon dioxide

B Starch

C Water

D Glucose

2. The diagram below shows a model cell that was set up to investigate diffusion through a selectively permeable membrane.

Iodine is a small, soluble molecule.

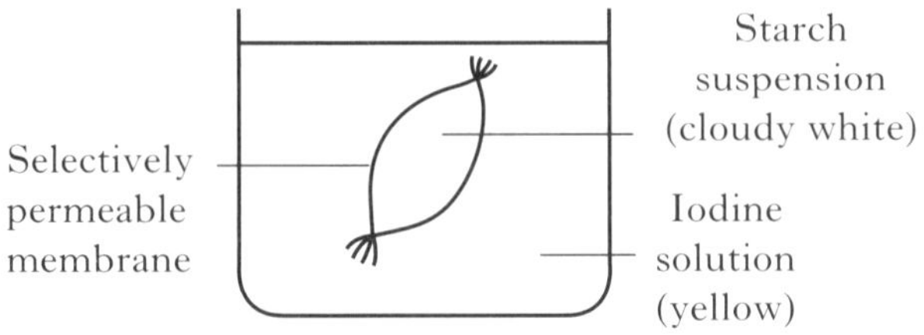

Predict the colour changes which would be observed after one hour.

	Colour change after one hour	
	Starch suspension	*Iodine solution*
A	remained cloudy white	yellow to blue/black
B	cloudy white to blue/black	remained yellow
C	remained cloudy white	remained yellow
D	cloudy white to blue/black	yellow to blue/black

3. The diagram below shows energy transfer within a cell.

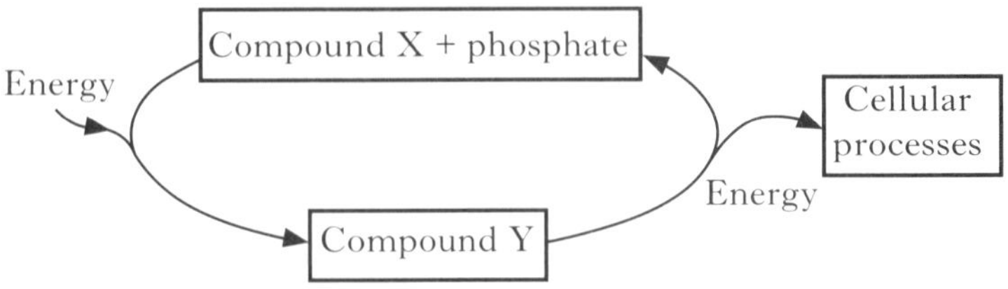

Which line in the table identifies correctly compounds X and Y?

	X	*Y*
A	glucose	CO_2
B	CO_2	ADP
C	ADP	ATP
D	ATP	glucose

4. Which of the following stages in respiration would result in the production of 38 molecules of ATP?

A Glucose to pyruvic acid

B Pyruvic acid to lactic acid

C Pyruvic acid to carbon dioxide and water

D Glucose to carbon dioxide and water

[Turn over

5. The diagrams below show four experiments used in an investigation into the conditions needed for photosynthesis.

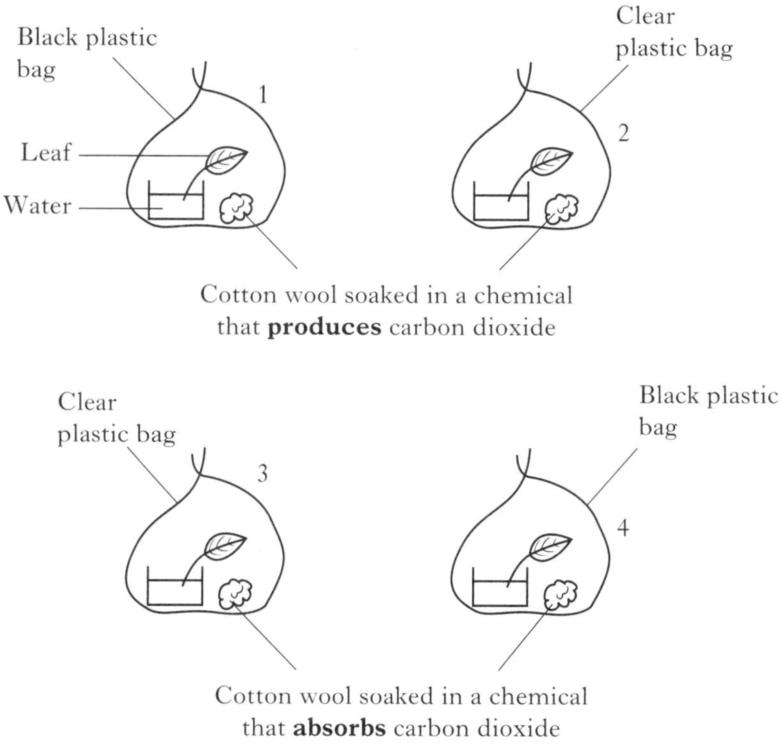

The results from which two experiments should be compared to show that light is needed for photosynthesis?

A 1 and 2

B 1 and 4

C 2 and 3

D 3 and 4

6. The graph below shows the rate of photosynthesis, as light intensity increases, at two different temperatures.

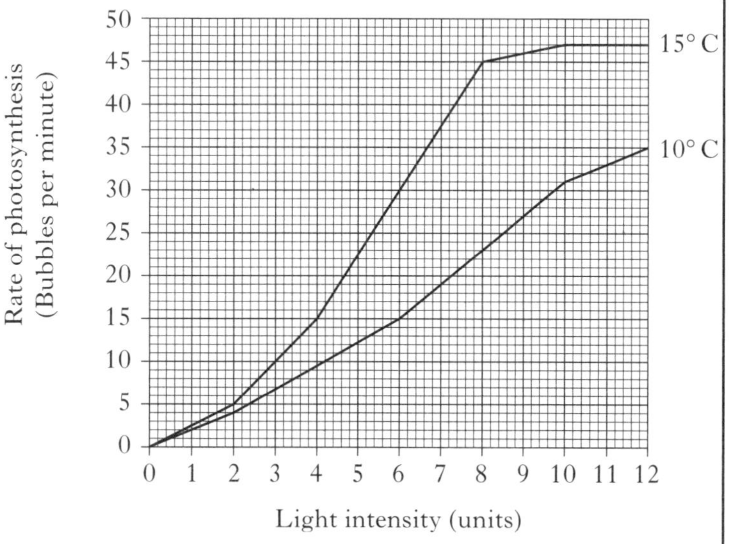

At a light intensity of 6 units, what is the simplest whole number ratio of the rate of photosynthesis at 10 °C compared to 15 °C?

A 15 : 30

B 10 : 15

C 3 : 6

D 1 : 2

7. A crop of tomatoes was grown in a polytunnel.

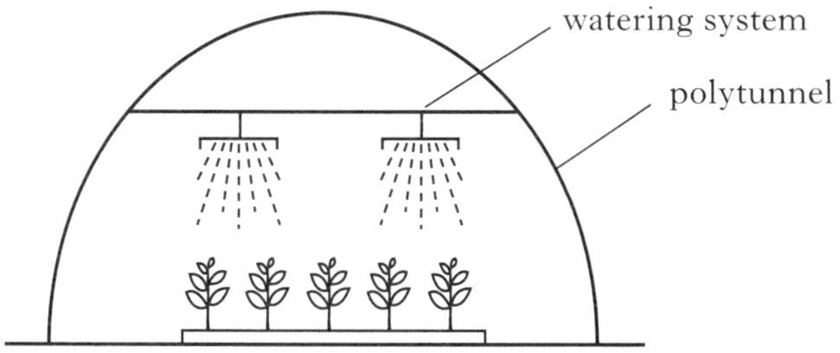

Which of the following changes would **not** produce an earlier crop of tomatoes?

A Increasing the heating during the day.

B Increasing the CO_2 concentration at night.

C Increasing the light intensity at night.

D Increasing the CO_2 concentration during the day.

8. An experiment was carried out to investigate the growth of plants for 40 days after germination.

The graph below shows the average dry mass of the plants.

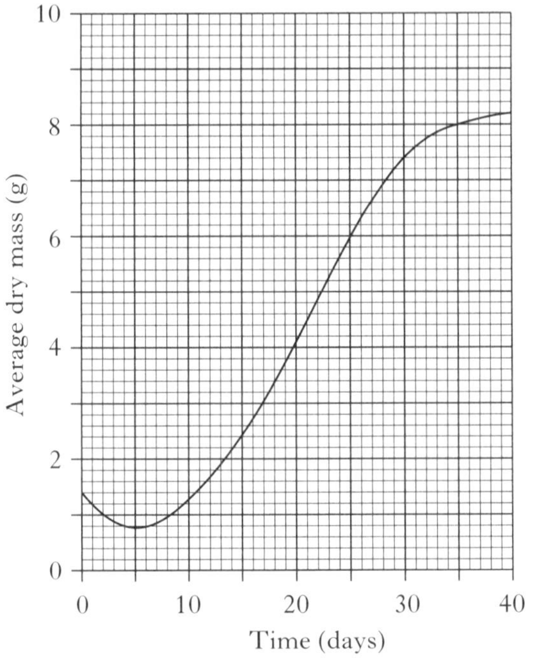

During which 5 day period is there the greatest increase in average dry mass?

A Days 5 – 10

B Days 10 – 15

C Days 20 – 25

D Days 25 – 30

9. The table below shows the results of an investigation into the effect of temperature on the number of eggs laid by female red spider mites.

	Temperature (°C)	
	20 °C	30 °C
Average number of eggs laid per female	90	60

The percentage decrease in the average number of eggs laid per female when the temperature is increased from 20 °C to 30 °C is

A 30%

B 33%

C 50%

D 67%.

10. A choice chamber was used to investigate the effect of humidity on the behaviour of woodlice, as shown below.

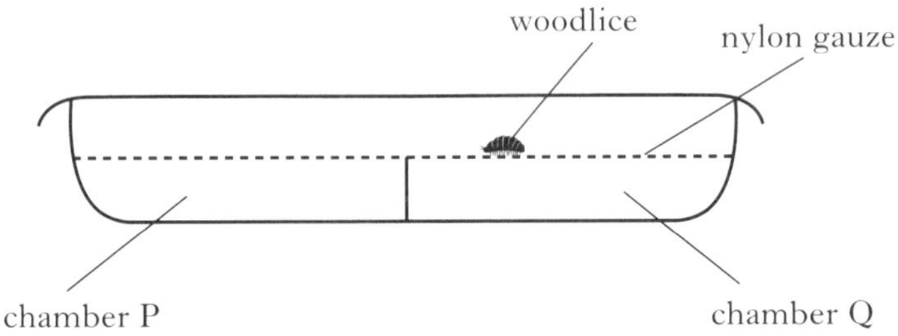

Which line in the table below describes the most appropriate set up for this investigation?

	Number of woodlice	*Contents of chamber P*	*Contents of chamber Q*	*Modification to choice chamber*
A	2	Drying agent	Wet cotton wool	Half covered in black paper
B	2	Wet cotton wool	Drying agent	Totally covered in black paper
C	10	Drying agent	Wet cotton wool	Half covered in black paper
D	10	Wet cotton wool	Drying agent	Totally covered in black paper

11. In corn on the cob, yellow seed (G) is dominant to purple seed (g). The cob shown below shows some yellow and some purple seeds. The seeds have been counted.

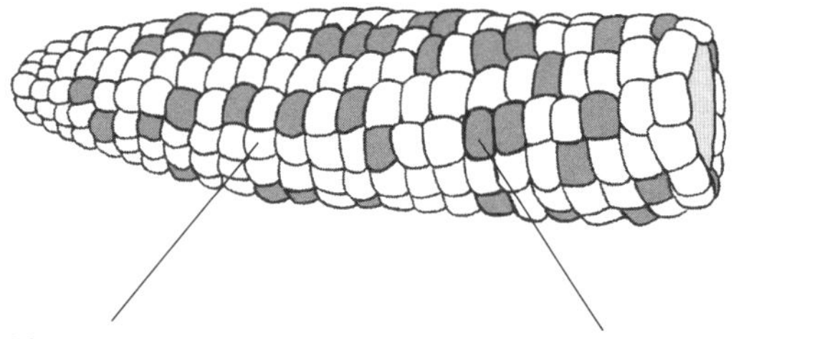

The genotypes of the parents that produced this cob were

A GG × gg

B Gg × gg

C gg × gg

D Gg × Gg.

12. The table below shows the relationship between planting density and the mass of seed harvested for a trial cereal crop.

Planting density (number of plants per square metre)	*Mass of seed harvested* (grammes per square metre)
4	60
8	86
15	105
32	77
128	21

The reason a low mass of seed was harvested when the planting density was 128 plants per square metre was

A less disease at high planting densities

B more nutrients available

C more competition for light and nutrients

D less space for weeds.

13. Which stage in the production of human insulin by genetic engineering is represented in the diagram below?

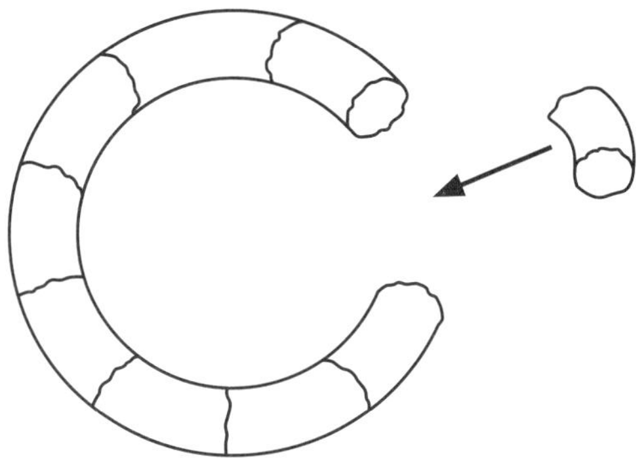

A Human gene is inserted into a plasmid.

B Human gene is inserted into a bacterium.

C Plasmid is inserted into a human chromosome.

D Bacterial gene is inserted into a human chromosome.

14. A hairy stemmed pea plant is crossed with a smooth stemmed pea plant. All the F_1 plants had hairy stems.

The genotype of the F_1 plants was

A heterozygous

B homozygous

C dominant

D recessive.

15. Differences in the mass of sunflower seeds are due to the interaction of the alleles of several genes.

This type of inheritance is called

A dominant

B monohybrid

C polygenic

D co-dominant.

16. Two groups of the seeds of genetically tall plants were grown under different conditions.

Group I seeds were grown in high light intensity and high nutrient levels.

Group II seeds were grown in low light intensity and low nutrient levels.

All plants in group I were taller than those in group II.

The effect of the different conditions on the phenotype is due to

A natural selection

B biodiversity

C environmental impact

D polygenic inheritance.

17. Which of the following is an example of selective breeding?

A Increasing milk yield in dairy cattle

B Industrial melanism in Peppered moths

C Insulin production by bacteria

D Insertion of DNA into a bacterium

18. Eight visking tubing (model gut) bags, as shown below, were placed into water baths.

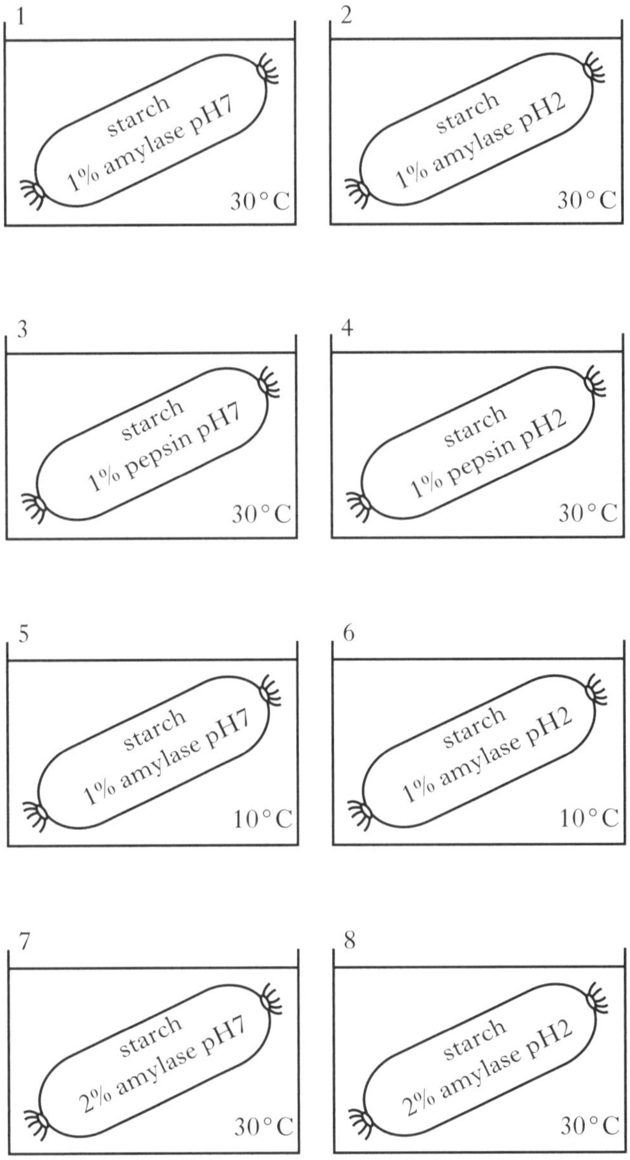

Which two bags could be compared to investigate the effect of pH on the digestion of starch?

A 1 and 4

B 2 and 5

C 2 and 7

D 7 and 8

[Turn over

19. The diagram below shows the human alimentary canal.

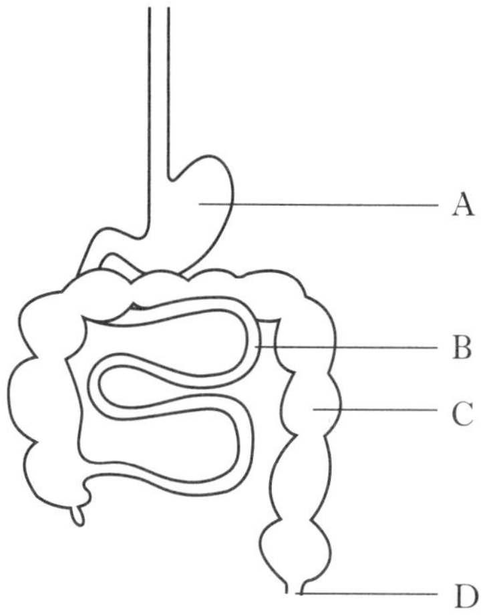

Which structure contains villi?

20. The diagram below shows the human urinary system.

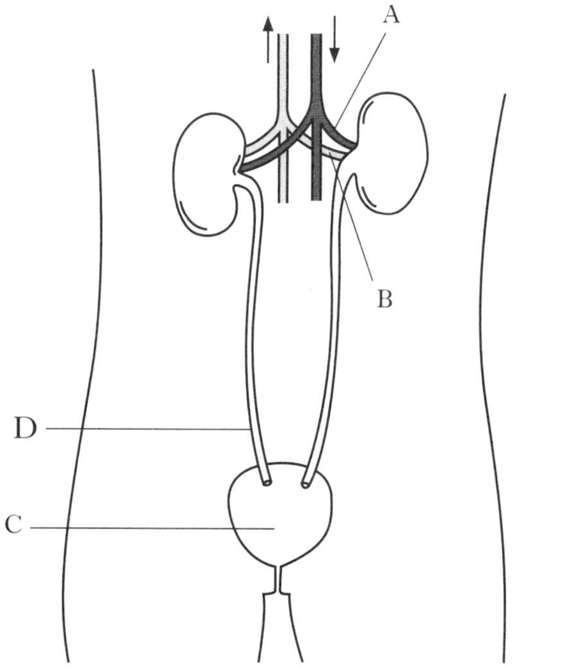

Which labelled part has the lowest concentration of urea?

21. A student has a heart rate of 80 beats per minute and a cardiac output of 4 litres per minute.

Cardiac output is calculated using the following equation:

Cardiac output = volume of blood per beat × heart rate

What is the volume of blood pumped per beat?

A 5 cm^3

B 20 cm^3

C 50 cm^3

D 320 cm^3

22. The diagram below shows the heart and circulation.

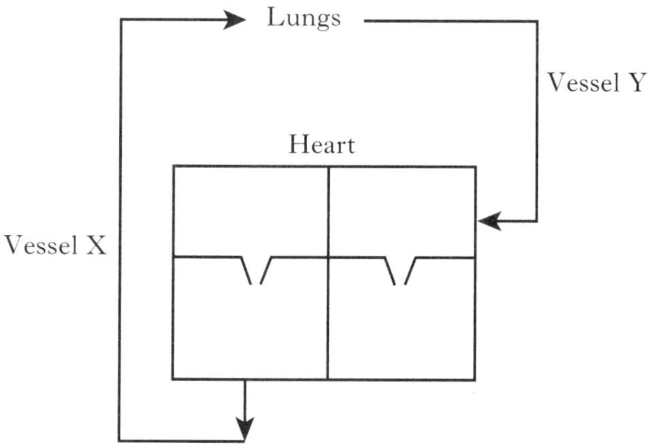

Which line in the table describes correctly the types of blood in vessels X and Y?

	Vessel X	*Vessel Y*
A	deoxygenated	deoxygenated
B	oxygenated	deoxygenated
C	oxygenated	oxygenated
D	deoxygenated	oxygenated

23. The list below refers to stages in the response of the nervous system to a stimulus.

1 Central nervous system sorts information.
2 Nerve impulses sent to muscles.
3 Nerve impulses sent to central nervous system.
4 Senses detect the stimulus.
5 Response is produced.

The correct order of the stages is

A $4 \rightarrow 3 \rightarrow 1 \rightarrow 2 \rightarrow 5$

B $3 \rightarrow 4 \rightarrow 2 \rightarrow 1 \rightarrow 5$

C $4 \rightarrow 3 \rightarrow 2 \rightarrow 1 \rightarrow 5$

D $3 \rightarrow 4 \rightarrow 1 \rightarrow 2 \rightarrow 5$.

24. The graph below shows the rates of water loss from an athlete when active and resting at different room temperatures.

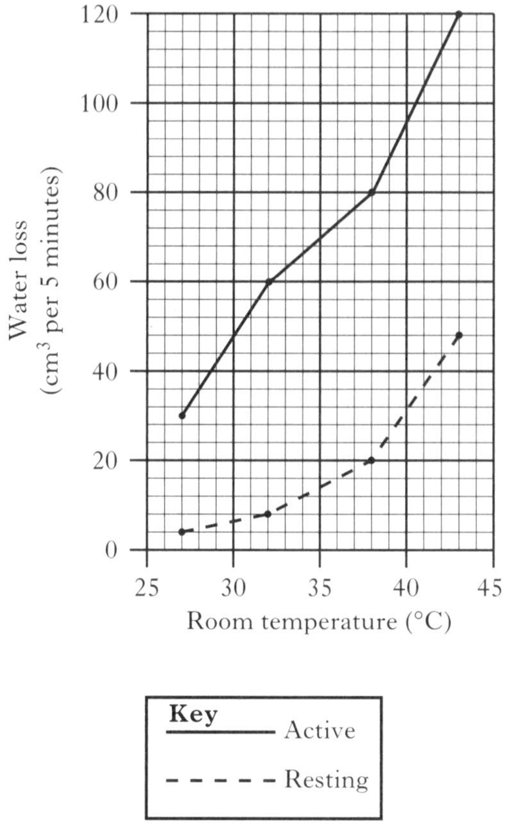

What is the difference in water loss per 5 minutes between active and resting at 43 °C?

A 70 cm^3

B 72 cm^3

C 76 cm^3

D 78 cm^3

25. Which of the following pathways shows the correct response in blood vessels of the skin to an increase in body temperature?

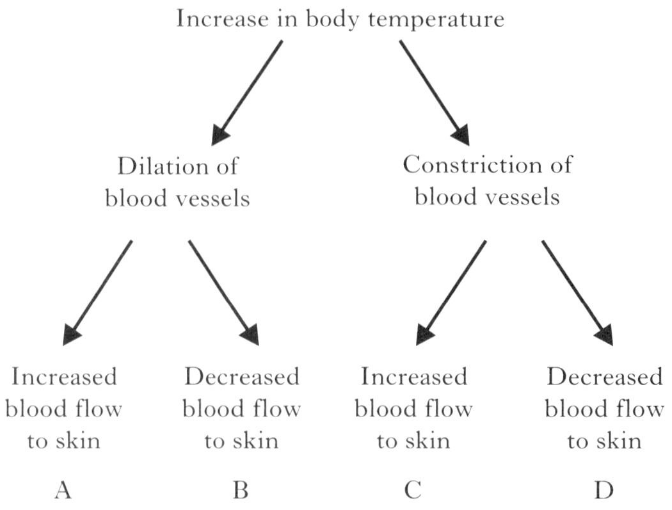

Candidates are reminded that the answer sheet for Section A MUST be placed INSIDE the front cover of this answer book.

DO NOT WRITE IN THIS MARGIN

Marks

SECTION B

All questions in this section should be attempted.
All answers must be written clearly and legibly in ink.

1. (*a*) The diagram below represents a potato cell.

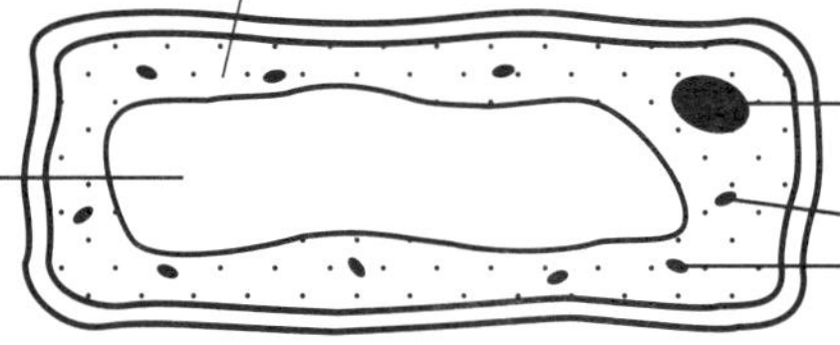

(i) Name the parts of the cell labelled X and Y.

X ____________________

Y ____________________ **1**

(ii) Give the function of structure Z.

____________________ **1**

(*b*) Name the enzyme involved in the synthesis of starch in potato cells.

____________________ **1**

(*c*) Give **one** difference and **one** similarity in the structure of plant and animal cells.

Difference ____________________

____________________ **1**

Similarity ____________________

____________________ **1**

DO NOT WRITE IN THIS MARGIN

Marks

2. (*a*) Yeast cells have many industrial and commercial uses.

The sentences below describe some of the uses of yeast cells.

Underline **one** option in each set of brackets to make the following sentences correct.

Yeast cells are {bacteria / fungi} that produce {carbon dioxide / oxygen} which makes bread rise. Yeast cells are also used in the production of {biogas / gasohol}. **2**

(*b*) Explain how milk is converted into yoghurt by bacteria.

____

____

____ **2**

[Turn over

DO NOT WRITE IN THIS MARGIN

Marks

3. An investigation was carried out to find the effect of salt solutions of different concentrations on the mass of potato tissue. Five test tubes were set up as shown below, each containing a different concentration of salt solution.

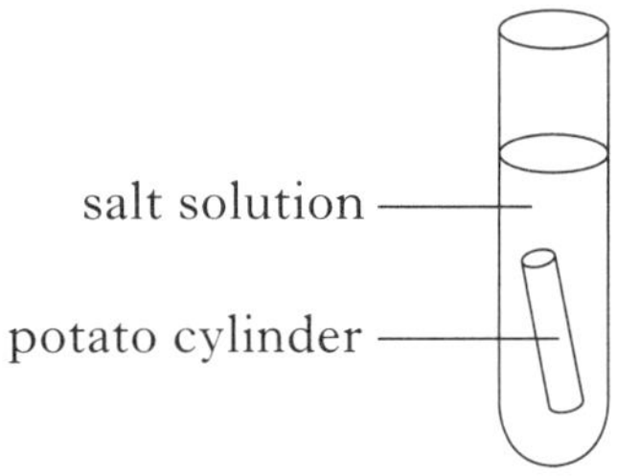

Each potato cylinder was weighed, placed in the solution and left for an hour. Each cylinder was then reweighed and the percentage (%) change in mass was calculated.

The table below shows the results of the investigation.

Salt concentration (g/100 cm^3)	*Change in mass* (%)
1	+15
3	+10
6	–5
8	–15
10	–20

(*a*) (i) Add the appropriate label to each axis. **1**

(ii) Construct a **line graph** using the results given in the table. **1**

(Additional graph paper, if required, will be found on *Page thirty*.)

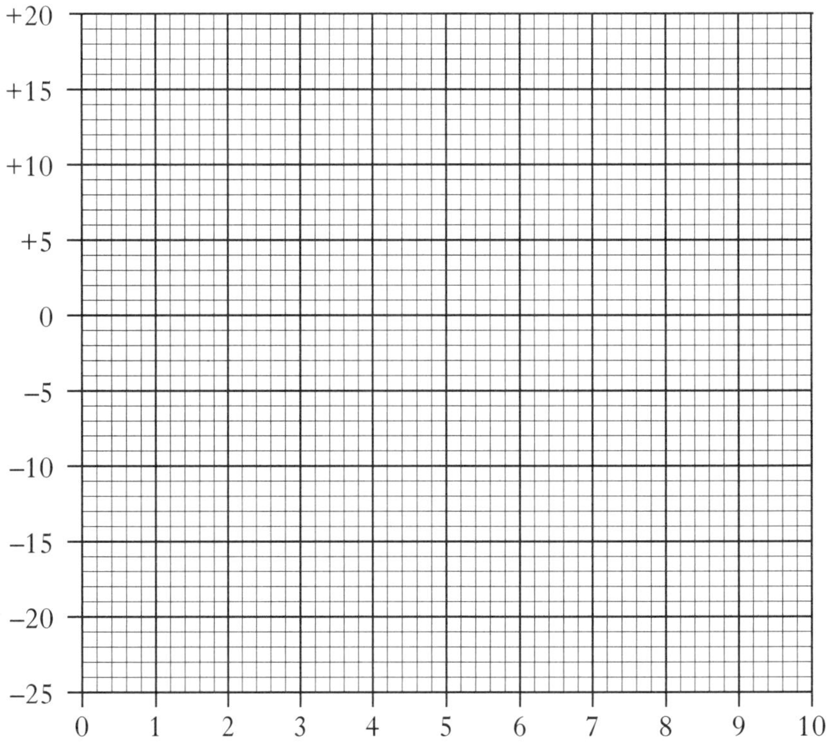

DO NOT WRITE IN THIS MARGIN

Marks

3. (continued)

(*b*) Time was kept constant in this investigation.

Name **two** other variables which must be kept constant.

1 ______________________________

2 ______________________________ **1**

(*c*) Using the results given, state the salt concentration which is isotonic to the potato tissue. Explain your answer.

Isotonic concentration ______________ $g/100\,cm^3$ **1**

Explanation ______________________________

______________________________ **1**

(*d*) Predict the salt concentration that would produce a 10% decrease in mass.

________ $g/100\,cm^3$ **1**

[Turn over

DO NOT WRITE IN THIS MARGIN

Marks

4. Enzymes are biological catalysts. The diagram below shows part of an enzyme controlled reaction.

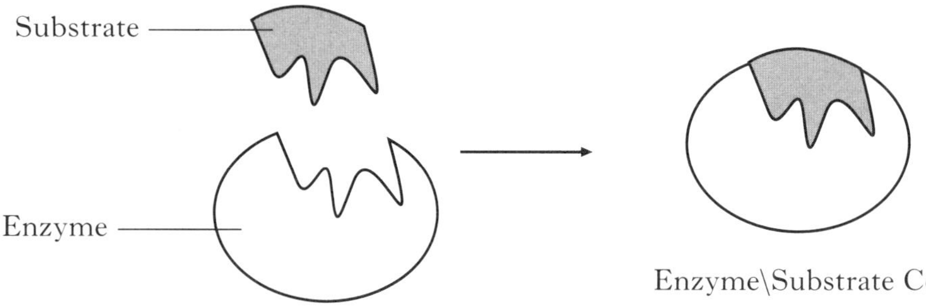

(*a*) Describe the features of an enzyme which allow it to combine with only one substrate.

____

____

____ **2**

(*b*) What happens to an enzyme when it is boiled?

____ **1**

(*c*) Name a factor, other than temperature, which affects enzyme activity.

____________________ **1**

(*d*) Complete the following word equation for the enzyme catalase.

hydrogen peroxide —catalase→ ______________ and ______________ **1**

substrate **products**

DO NOT WRITE IN THIS MARGIN

Marks

5. A study has shown that Scotland's river otter population is increasing after falling sharply over the last 40 years.

Otters live along the banks of rivers, usually in reeds and gaps between tree roots. Fish are their main food.

(*a*) What term is used for the place where otters live?

______________________________ **1**

(*b*) What disadvantage might otters have if reeds are removed from riverbanks?

____

______________________________ **1**

(*c*) Mink are North American animals introduced into Scotland. They feed on fish and live in riverbanks.

What effect would the mink have on otter numbers? Explain your answer.

Effect ______________________________

Explanation ______________________________

______________________________ **2**

(*d*) An ecosystem such as the otters' has several components.

Complete the table below to identify the terms used and their definitions.

Term	*Definition*
	A green plant that makes its own food.
Carnivore	
Community	

2

DO NOT WRITE IN THIS MARGIN

Marks

6. Boll weevil insects, shown in the picture below, feed on cotton plants. There are two varieties of cotton plant, original variety (V) and boll weevil resistant variety (R).

Three farms were used to compare the yield of the two varieties. Each farmer planted two fields, one of each variety. All fields were treated identically. The yield of cotton from each field was weighed. The results are shown in the bar graph below.

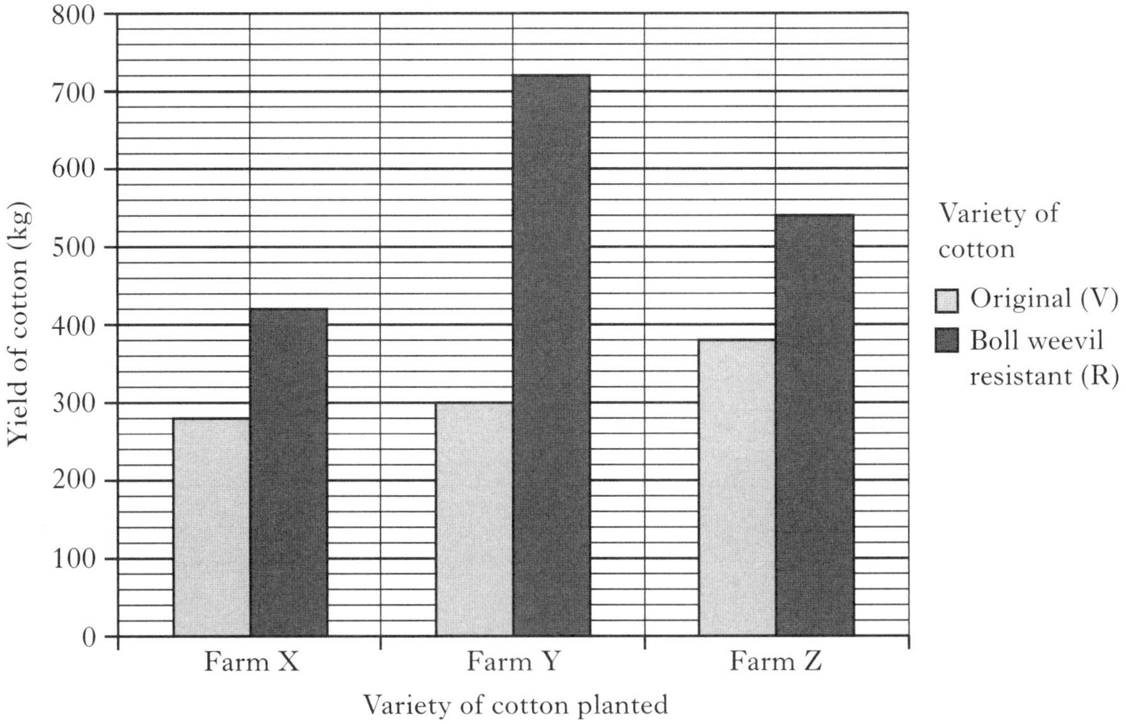

(*a*) Calculate the average yield of V cotton.

Space for calculation

_______________ kg **1**

DO NOT WRITE IN THIS MARGIN

Marks

6. (continued)

(*b*) Calculate the percentage difference in yield between the two varieties of cotton grown at Farm X.

Space for calculation

____________ % **1**

(*c*) (i) Name the variable altered in this investigation.

____ **1**

(ii) The fields planted with V cotton were used as a control.

Give a reason for using this control.

____

____ **1**

(iii) Explain why using ten farms instead of three would have improved this investigation.

____ **1**

(*d*) What conclusion can be drawn from these results?

____

____ **1**

(*e*) The farmers use pesticides to kill insects which damage their crops.

(i) Explain why less pesticide is needed when growing R cotton.

____

____ **1**

(ii) Explain why growing R cotton is less likely to affect insect biodiversity.

____

____ **1**

[Turn over

DO NOT WRITE IN THIS MARGIN

Marks

7. (*a*) Hair appearance in mice is controlled by a single gene.

Wavy hair (H) is dominant to straight hair (h).

Two homozygous mice were crossed, one had wavy hair and one had straight hair.

(i) Complete the genotypes of the parental generation (P).

Wavy haired × **Straight haired**

P genotypes ____________ × ____________ **1**

(ii) State the phenotype of the F_1 mice.

F_1 phenotype ______________________________ **1**

(iii) An F_1 mouse was crossed with a straight haired mouse.

State the genotype of the wavy haired offspring.

Space for working

Genotype ______________________________ **1**

(*b*) What term is used to describe alleles which are neither dominant nor recessive?

____ **1**

(*c*) The sentence below describes the function of DNA.

Underline **one** option in each set of brackets to make the following sentence correct.

The {number / order} of DNA {bases / genes} in a chromosome encodes information

for the structure of a {carbohydrate / protein}. **2**

DO NOT WRITE IN THIS MARGIN

Marks

8. (*a*) Name **two** places in the alimentary canal where protein is digested.

1 ______________________________

2 ______________________________ **2**

(*b*) The nutrition information panel below is from a chocolate bar.

Each bar contains . . .			
Calories 170 8·5%	**Sugars** 17·7 g 19·6%	**Fat** 9·9 g 14·1%	**Saturates** 6·6 g 10·4%
of your guideline daily amount			

(i) According to this information, how many calories make up your guideline daily amount?

Space for calculation

______________ calories **1**

(ii) Saturates are a type of fat which form part of the total fat (9·9 g) in this chocolate bar.

What percentage of the total fat is saturates?

Space for calculation

______________% **1**

[Turn over

Marks

9. The diagram below shows an investigation into the effect of pH on the digestion of protein by trypsin.

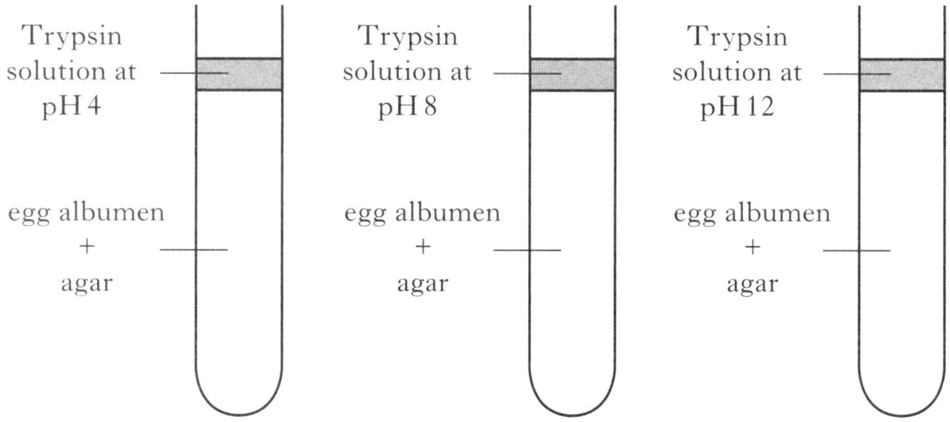

Egg albumen is the source of protein. It is added to agar to give a cloudy, white jelly. When the egg albumen is digested the jelly turns clear.

The test tubes were left in a warm place for 24 hours. At the end of this time the depth of the clear jelly was measured.

The graph below shows results from this investigation.

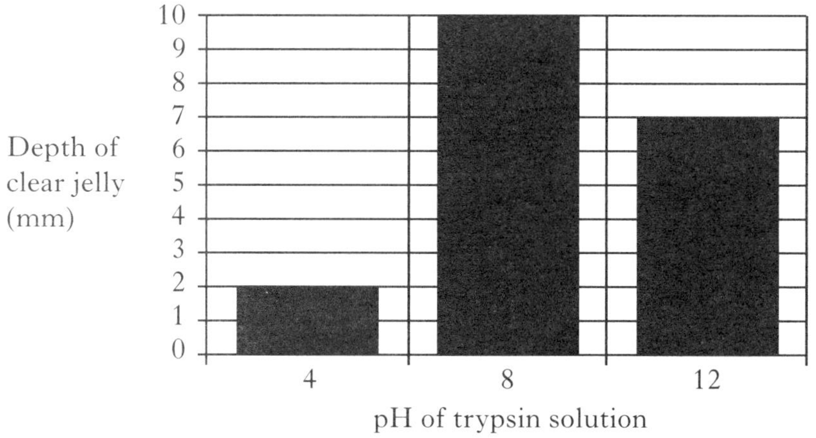

(*a*) Describe trypsin activity as pH increases as shown in the graph.

____

____

____ **2**

DO NOT WRITE IN THIS MARGIN

Marks

9. (continued)

(*b*) Predict the depth of clear jelly with trypsin at pH 2.

______________ mm **1**

(*c*) Trypsin is produced by the pancreas. Name **two** other enzymes produced by the pancreas.

1 __________________________________ **1**

2 __________________________________ **1**

[Turn over

DO NOT WRITE IN THIS MARGIN

Marks

10. (*a*) Marine bony fish are found in the North Sea.

Underline **one** option in each set of brackets to make the following sentences correct.

Marine bony fish have tissues that are { hypertonic / hypotonic } to sea water.

They overcome osmotic problems by { absorbing / excreting } salts and producing

{ concentrated / dilute } urine. **2**

(*b*) The diagram below shows part of a nephron from a human kidney.

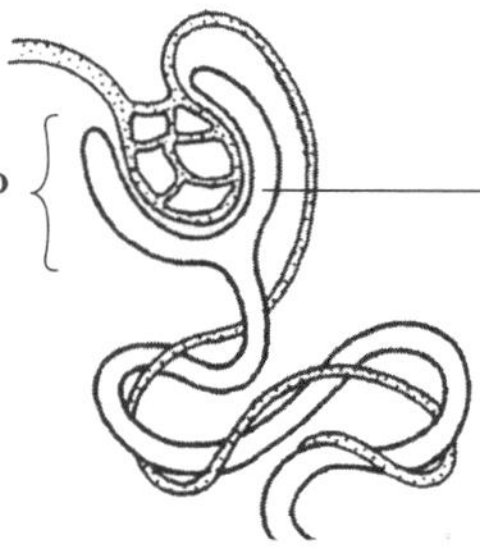

(i) Name structure Q.

____ **1**

(ii) Name the process carried out at P.

____ **1**

(*c*) The hormone ADH affects water reabsorption from the nephron.

(i) Which part of the brain releases ADH?

____ **1**

(ii) Name a part of a nephron where water is reabsorbed.

____ **1**

DO NOT WRITE IN THIS MARGIN

Marks

11. The diagram below shows an alveolus and a capillary in the lungs where gas exchange occurs.

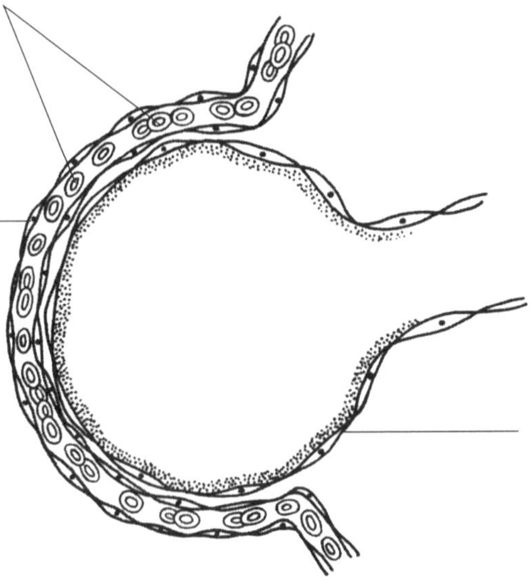

(*a*) Decide if each of the following statements about gas exchange is **True** or **False**, and tick (✓) the appropriate box.

If the statement is **False**, write the correct word(s) in the **Correction** box to replace the word underlined in the statement.

Statement	*True*	*False*	*Correction*
Lungs have a <u>large</u> surface area for efficient gas exchange.			
The thin walls of alveoli <u>slow down</u> gas exchange.			
There is a lower <u>oxygen</u> concentration in the alveoli than in the blood.			

3

(*b*) How is oxygen carried in the red blood cells?

____ **1**

(*c*) Blood plasma transports the blood cells.

Name **two** other substances carried by the blood plasma.

____________________ and ____________________ **1**

[Turn over

DO NOT WRITE IN THIS MARGIN

Marks

12. (*a*) Different parts of the brain have different functions.

Draw **one** line to link each part of the brain with its correct function. (One example has been completed for you.)

Part of the brain		*Function*
Cerebrum		regulation of temperature
Medulla	————————	control of breathing rate
Cerebellum		conscious responses
Hypothalamus		co-ordination of movement

2

(*b*) (i) The flow chart below shows the structures in a reflex arc.

Complete the chart by inserting the names of the missing neurones.

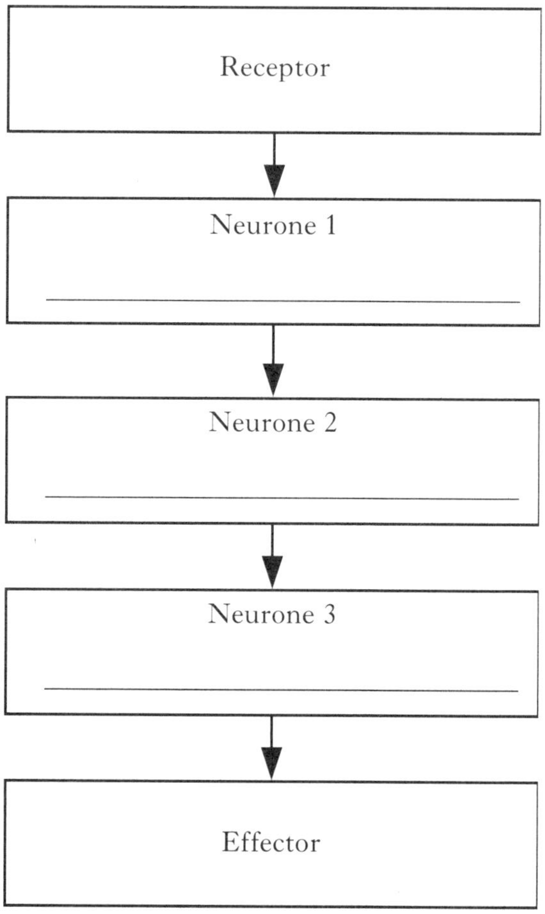

2

(ii) Describe a function of a reflex response.

____

______________________________ **1**

[Turn over for Section C on *Page twenty-six*

SECTION C

Marks

Both questions in this section should be attempted.

Note that each question contains a choice.

Questions 1 and 2 should be attempted on the blank pages which follow.
All answers must be written clearly and legibly in ink.

Supplementary sheets, if required, may be obtained from the Invigilator.

1. Answer **either** A **or** B.

A. The pictures below show a food chain which is also represented by two types of pyramid.

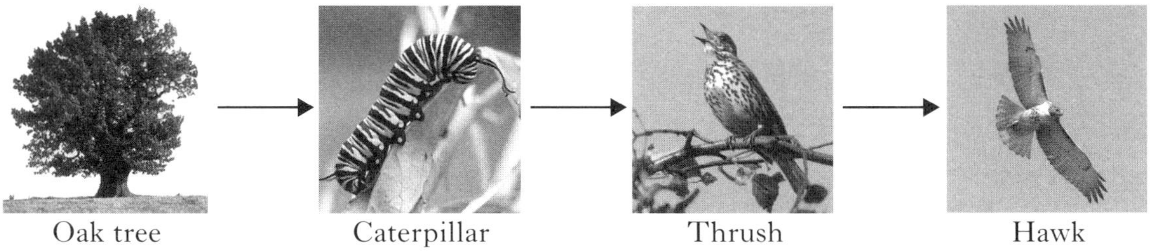

Name the type of pyramid X. Explain why **both** pyramids are correct for this food chain. **5**

OR

B. The diagram below represents some of the stages of meiosis in the testes.

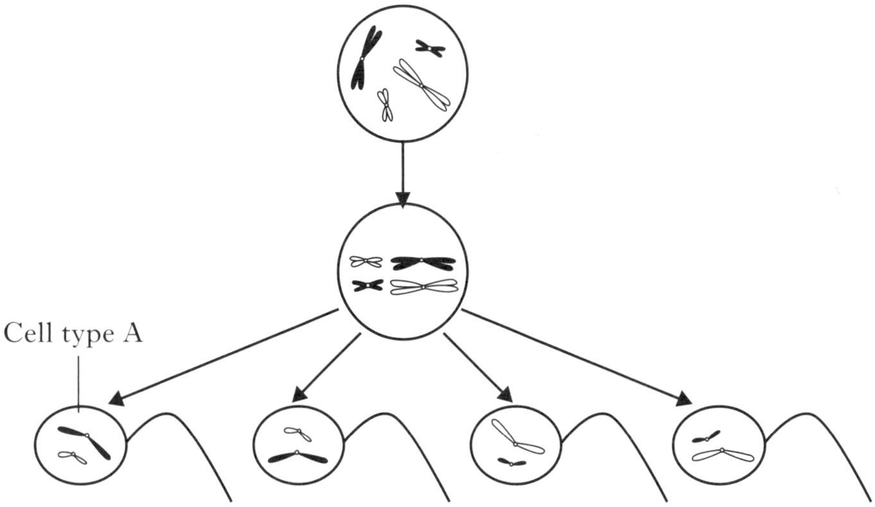

Name cell type A **and** describe the role of **both** meiosis and fertilisation in producing offspring. **5**

Question 2 is on *Page twenty-eight*.

DO NOT WRITE IN THIS MARGIN

SPACE FOR ANSWER TO QUESTION 1

[Turn over for Question 2 on *Page twenty-eight*

DO NOT WRITE IN THIS MARGIN

Marks

2. Answer **either** A **or** B.

Labelled diagrams may be included where appropriate.

A. Describe the **two** stages of aerobic respiration **including** the names of the raw materials and products for **each** stage. 5

OR

B. Describe the **two** stages of photosynthesis **including** the names of the raw materials and products for **each** stage. 5

[END OF QUESTION PAPER]

DO NOT WRITE IN THIS MARGIN

SPACE FOR ANSWER TO QUESTION 2

DO NOT WRITE IN THIS MARGIN

ADDITIONAL SPACE FOR ANSWERS

ADDITIONAL GRAPH PAPER FOR QUESTION 3(*a*)

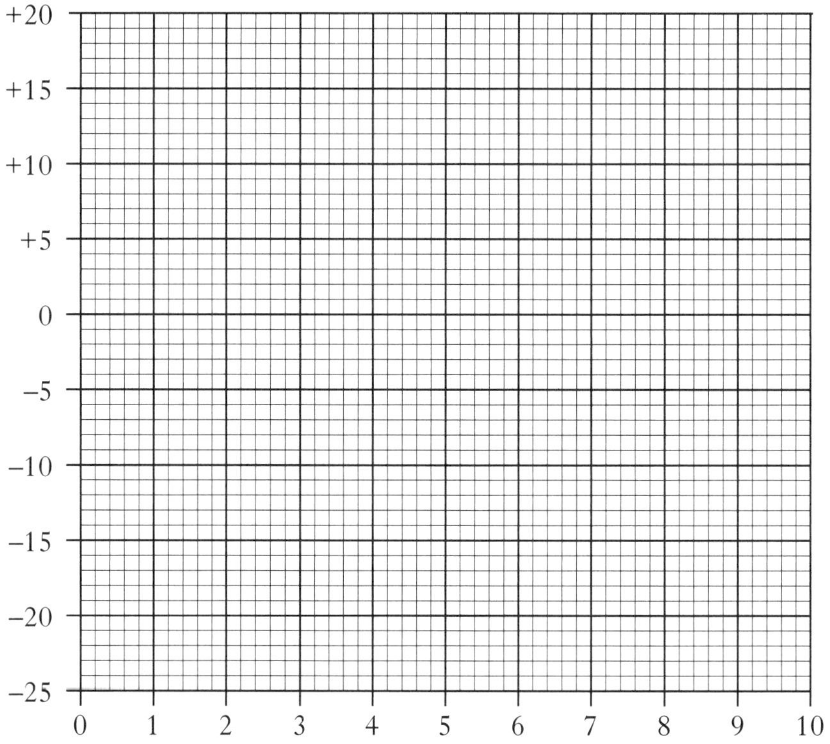

INTERMEDIATE 2 | ANSWER SECTION

BrightRED ANSWER SECTION FOR

SQA INTERMEDIATE 2 BIOLOGY 2007–2011

BIOLOGY INTERMEDIATE 2 2007

SECTION A

1. C	**11.** A	**21.** D
2. D	**12.** B	**22.** B
3. A	**13.** D	**23.** C
4. C	**14.** B	**24.** C
5. B	**15.** B	**25.** B
6. C	**16.** D	
7. D	**17.** C	
8. B	**18.** A	
9. D	**19.** D	
10. A	**20.** A	

SECTION B

1. (*a*) trachea / artery / left

(*b*) *Any two from:*
- thin/one cell thick/(semi) permeable lining/wall
- moist
- large surface area
- good blood supply **or** many blood capillaries **or** in close contact with blood capillaries

(*c*) (i) glucose
(ii) carbon dioxide/water/lactic acid

(*d*) (i) water
(ii) Turgid/hypertonic

2. (*a*) (i)
- To make sure no other factor is producing the result **or**
- to show it is the germinating/live peas that are producing the result **or**
- to show it is the germinating/live peas that are using oxygen **or**
- for a valid conclusion

(ii) It/The liquid will rise more quickly/higher.

(*b*)

Aerobic respiration in germinating peas	*Anaerobic respiration in germinating peas*
X Y	W X Z

3. (*a*) (i) green/yellow/orange/red/brown
(ii) Protein

(*b*) **Box 1** - amino acids
Box 2 - carbon, hydrogen, oxygen/CHO

(*c*) (i) pepsin/rennin
(ii) 1·4 to 1·6 is acceptable

4. (*a*) (i) 5·5
(ii)
- concentration of hydrogen peroxide **or**
- pH (of hydrogen peroxide) **or**
- mass/surface area/volume of tissue/cube **or**
- temperature

(iii) repeated (and average calculated)

(iv)
- different tissues have different catalase concentrations **or**
- liver has the most catalase **or**
- apple has the least catalase

(*b*) (i) synthesis
(ii) increases/speeds it up/faster
(iii)
- lipase/not specific to glucose-1-phosphate **or**
- lipase/active site does not fit glucose-1-phosphate **or**
- lipase is specific to fats **or**
- only phosphorylase is specific to glucose-1-phosphate **or**
- an enzyme is specific to its substrate/reaction

5. (*a*)

Structure	*Letter*	*Function*
Bladder	E	**Stores/holds urine**
Renal artery	A	Carries blood into the kidney
Ureter	**D**	Carries urine away from the kidney

(*b*) (i) ADH/anti diuretic (hormone)
(ii) decreases/reduces/less
(iii) glucose and salts
(iv) 60

6. (*a*) **P** sensory
Q motor

(*b*) (eyelid) muscles

(*c*) for protection **or** rapid/fast/quick

7. (*a*) (i) oxygen
(ii) **A**
NB Graph line should not extend to the origin or past the last point

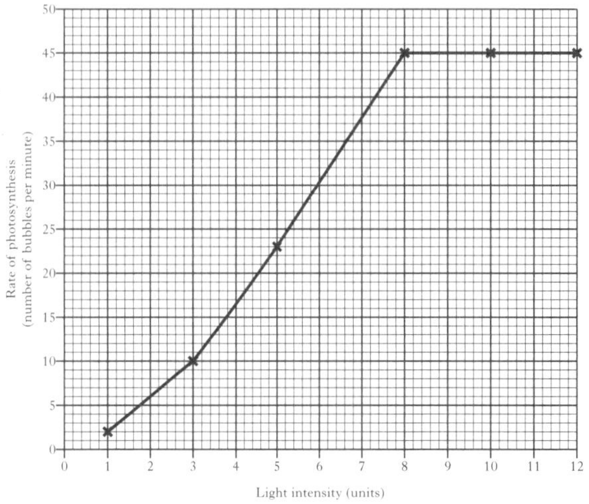

B Another factor is limiting (photosynthesis) **or**
It has reached the optimum/maximum rate for these conditions **or**
Light is no longer a limiting factor

(*b*) (i) **Substance 1** - ATP
Substance 2 - hydrogen/$NADPH_{(2)}$

(ii) carbon fixation/Calvin cycle

(*c*)

Role of carbohydrate in plant cells	*Name of carbohydrate*
Storage as an insoluble material	**starch**
Forms cell walls	**cellulose**

8. (*a*) (i) nucleus

(ii) **A** DNA/deoxyribonucleic acid

B *Any two from:*

It/DNA determines the sequence of amino acids in enzyme/protein **or**

It/DNA determines the structure/ function/type of enzyme/protein **or** Enzymes/proteins control cell activities.

(*b*) (i) Meiosis

(ii) Random/independent assortment

(iii) Half / fusion / twice

9. (*a*) (i) (Cross) 1 / F_1

(ii)

		Genotypes of gametes of Cross 2 single comb parent	
		r	**r**
Genotypes of gametes of Cross 2 rose comb parent	R	**Rr**	**Rr**
	r	**rr**	**rr**

(*b*)

Statement	*True*	*False*	*Correction*
co-dominant		✓	polygenic
gene	✓		
homozygous	✓		

10. (*a*) Jan to Apr - decreases
Apr to Aug - increases
Aug to Dec - decreases
(Figure and unit used at least once)

(*b*) 6

(*c*) No/fewer predators/birds from April to August **or** They have reproduced from April to August

(*d*)
- *If answer is decreases*:
  Corophium will become extinct **or** reduced number of Corophium leads to reduced number of predator species **or**
- *If answer is stays the same*:
  No species become extinct (only population falls) **or**
- *If answer is increases*:
  Less Corophium means less competition, therefore more species move in

SECTION C

1 A. (*a*) A1 red blood cells and plasma

(*b*) *Maximum of four from:*

A2 oxygen transported in red blood cells
A3 attached to haemoglobin/as oxyhaemoglobin
A4 carbon dioxide transported in red blood cells/attached to haemoglobin
A5 carbon dioxide carried in/dissolved in plasma
A6 carried as bicarbonate ions
A7 soluble foods dissolved in plasma
A8 named example of soluble food carried
A9 other correct substance carried by plasma, eg water/hormones/vitamins/minerals/salts/fats/proteins

1 B. (*a*) B1 hypothalamus

(*b*) *Maximum of four from:*

B2 sweating is reduced/stops
B3 blood vessels constrict/narrow/vasoconstriction
B4 reduces blood flow (to skin)
B5 to reduce heat loss
B6 hair stands on end/hair (erector) muscles contract
B7 to trap air/heat/insulate
B8 rapid/quick/repeated muscle contraction/shivering
B9 to generate heat/increase (body) temperature/heat up

2 A. A1 (Insulin) gene identified/located
A2 (Insulin) gene removed from human chromosome
A3 Plasmid removed from bacterium
A4 Plasmid cut open
A5 Enzyme(s) used
A6 (Insulin) gene inserted into plasmid
A7 Plasmid inserted into bacterium
A8 Bacteria multiply/cultured
A9 Bacteria produce insulin
A10 Insulin extracted/purified for use

2 B. B1 Two forms found
B2 Dark form occurs naturally/by mutation
B3 In rural/non-polluted areas trees covered in lichen/light coloured
B4 In industrial/polluted areas trees covered in soot/dark coloured
B5 Example of which form is most/least common linked to its environment
B6 Camouflage (not active, eg moths camouflage themselves)
B7 Seen/eaten by predators/birds (any correct example)
B8 Chances of survival
B9 Chances of breeding
B10 Chances of passing on their characteristics/genes to the next generation
B11 Description of population change

BIOLOGY INTERMEDIATE 2 2008

SECTION A

1. A	**11.** B	**21.** A
2. C	**12.** C	**22.** B
3. B	**13.** A	**23.** A
4. C	**14.** D	**24.** D
5. D	**15.** B	**25.** D
6. C	**16.** B	
7. A	**17.** D	
8. A	**18.** C	
9. C	**19.** B	
10. D	**20.** B	

SECTION B

1. (*a*) (i)

Structure	*Function*
(cell) membrane	controls the entry and exit of materials
cytoplasm	***site of chemical reactions/cell activities***
nucleus	***controls/stores genetic information/controls cell activities***

(ii) chloroplasts

(*b*) cellulose

2. (*a*) oxygen

(*b*) (i) ATP

(ii) combines with carbon dioxide

(*c*) (i) temperature affects the activity of enzymes; activity of enzymes affects the rate of photosynthesis/carbon fixation temperature dependent

(ii) carbon dioxide (concentration) light (intensity)

3. (*a*) (i) A glucose
B water
C ADP

(ii) muscular contraction
maintaining body temperature
cell division
transmission of nerve impulses
glycolysis
carbon fixation (any one)

(*b*) oxygen debt is repaid/(lactic acid is) converted into pyruvic acid

4. (*a*) −15% (minus sign must be included)

(*b*) (i) sugar concentration

(ii) Repeat the experiment (several times)

(iii) NOT VALID ticked and any one from:
to prevent introducing another variable;
(to remove) excess/surface water which would affect mass/results

(*c*) (i) C / D / E

(ii) smaller/flaccid/softer/wrinkled/shrunken

5. (*a*) (i)

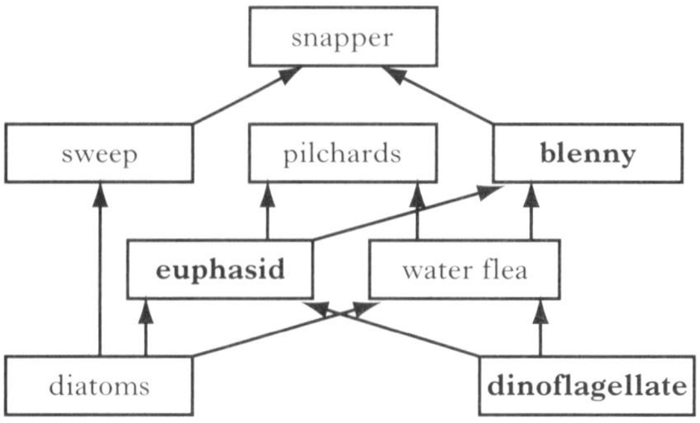

(ii) carnivore/predator/consumer (not primary)

(*b*) *Effect:* decrease
Explanation: due to more pilchards and blenny to eat them
or
due to more sweep so less diatoms as food

6. (*a*) (i)

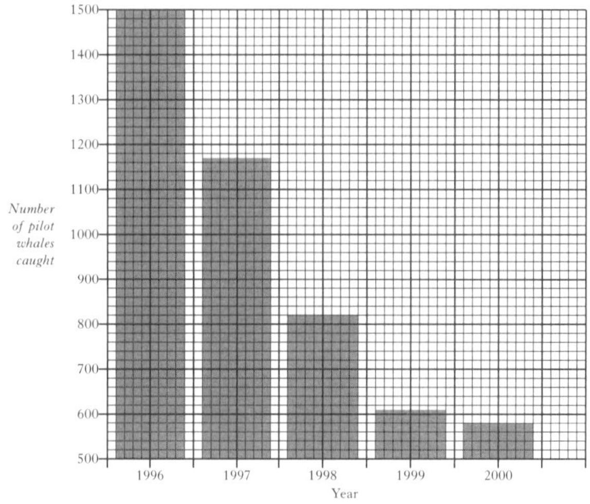

(ii) (as the years pass) the catches fall/decrease

(iii) 936

(*b*) 1·25 times

7. (*a*) (i) BB bb

(ii) Bb

(iii) blue

(*b*)

		Genotype of ganetes from F_1 parent	
		B	b
Genotype of ganetes from yellow parent	b	Bb	bb
	(b)	(Bb)	(bb)

8. (*a*) (i) *Any one from:*
different foods
feed at different heights
only zebra can feed on grass
(some comparison needed)

(ii) *Any one from:*

- long/deep roots/shallow/extensive roots
- reduced leaf surface area
- thick waxy cuticle
- succulent tissue
- needles/spines

(*b*) due to **very** high levels of grazing/overgraze/eat everything number of (grass) species reduced

9. (*a*) X tricuspid/AV
Y (left) ventricle

(*b*)

Statement	T/F	Correction
Capillaries contain valves.	**False**	**veins**
Veins allow gas exchange.	**False**	**capillaries**
Blood leaves the heart in arteries.	**True**	

(*c*) Oygen is transported by red blood cells. It combines with haemoglobin to form oxyhaemoglobin at high oxygen levels. Antibodies are produced by lymphocytes.

10. (*a*) (i) 2·25 – 2·3

(ii) *Any two from:*

- vasodilation/increased blood flow to skin
- increased heat loss/radiation
- sweating
- hairs lie flat

(*b*) (i) hypothalamus

(ii) negative feedback

(iii) sensory nerves/neurones

or

as electrical/nerve impulses

11. (*a*) (i) 80

(ii) none in renal vein/none reabsorbed high concentration in ureter

(iii) water

(*b*) *Process 1:* (ultra) filtration

Process 2: reabsorption (or reverse order)

(*c*) *Problem:* influx of water/water gain

Method: produce large volume of urine/ dilute urine/increase filtration/reduced reabsorption many (large) glomeruli

12. (*a*) (i) (A) hepatic portal vein

(B) broken down to form urea

or deamination to form urea

(ii) (A) gall bladder

(B) emulsifies fat/neutralise stomach contents

(*b*)

Enzyme	*Substrate*	*Product*
Trypsin/ protease	protein	**amino acids/(poly) peptides**
amylase	**starch**	maltose

SECTION C

1 **A.** *Maximum of two from:*

A1 anthers produce pollen grains

A2 ovaries produce ovules

Maximum of two from:

A3 gametes formed by meiosis

A4 two sets of chromosomes to one set/haploid cells form/chromosome number halved

A5 4 gametes formed (from one cell)

Maximum of two from:

A6 pollen tube (any correct description)

A7 fertilisation restores two sets of chromosomes/diploid cells

A8 male gamete/pollen fuses with female gamete/ovule

A9 fusion of nuclei

A10 form zygote

1 **B.** *Maximum of two from:*

B1 bacterial cell/bacteria = A

B2 medicines for human use/insulin/human growth hormone/Factor VIII

Advantages

Maximum of two from:

B3 increased range of products

B4 increased rate of production/product volume/decreased cost of production

B5 increase product purity

B6 an example of moral/ethical (can be awarded in either advantages or disadvantages)

Disadvantages

Maximum of two from:

B7 risk of release of genetically engineered bacteria into environment

B8 cost of development

B9 transfer of antibiotic resistance/other similar example

2 **A.** *Maximum of two from:*

A1 yeast contains enzymes (for anaerobic respiration)

A2 yeast ferment sugar/glucose

A3 carbon dioxide produced

A4 (CO_2) makes dough/bread rise

Maximum of three from:

A5 in the absence of oxygen

A6 (first stage) glycolysis occurs

A7 glucose converted into pyruvic acid(s)

A8 pyruvic acid is broken down

A9 to ethanol/alcohol and carbon dioxide

A10 anaerobic conversion is irreversible

A11 (glycolysis/glucose breakdown) produces 2 ATP

A12 enzymes used for anaerobic respiration

2 **B.** *Maximum of three from:*

B1 (enzymes are) composed of proteins

B2 (enzymes are) catalysts/speed up reactions/ lower the energy required for a reaction to take place

B3 (enzymes) can be reused/(enzymes) are unchanged in the reaction

B4 they have an active site

B5 specific substrate fits into enzyme/enzyme-substrate complex/lock and key/complementary/suitable labelled diagram/enzymes are specific or example

B6 any correct point about temperature/pH affecting enzyme activity/structure

Maximum of two from:

B7 glucose-1-phosphate/G-1-P is the substrate

B8 starch is the product/is made

B9 small/simple molecules to large/complex molecules

BIOLOGY INTERMEDIATE 2 2009

SECTION A

1. A	**11.** C	**21.** C
2. A	**12.** B	**22.** A
3. C	**13.** D	**23.** B
4. A	**14.** C	**24.** D
5. A	**15.** C	**25.** D
6. C	**16.** D	
7. B	**17.** C	
8. D	**18.** B	
9. B	**19.** A	
10. D	**20.** D	

SECTION B

1. (*a*) (i) YZX

(ii) 3

(*b*) protein

(*c*) (The active site/enzyme/it) is altered/changes shape/structure becomes deformed **or**
No longer specific/fits its substrate **or**
Stops working/becomes inactive

2. (*a*) (pH) 9

(*b*) pH

(*c*) Makes the results more reliable
To minimise unusual/atypical results

(*d*)

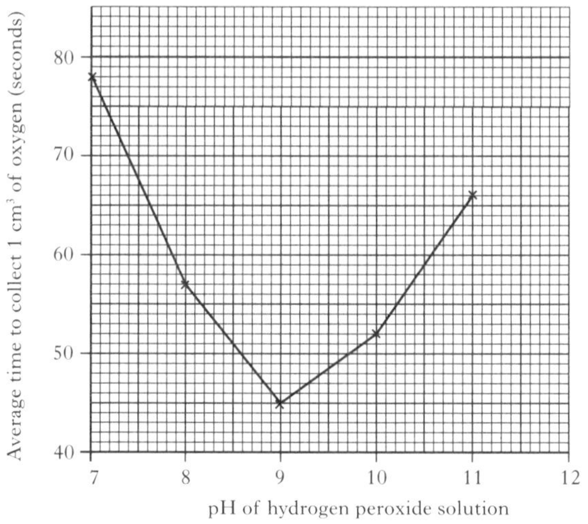

(*e*) 67 - 87

3. (*a*) aerobic

(*b*) (i) X = pyruvic acid/pyruvate
Y = ATP

(ii) Oxygen

(*c*) (i) Anaerobic/fermentation

(ii) produces alcohol/ethanol

4. (*a*) (i) 5%

(ii) Only ATP causes muscle/tissue to contract

(*b*) (i) (muscle) fatigue

(ii) it is changed back into pyruvic acid **or**
repay oxygen debt **or**
more oxygen to tissue/muscle/it

5. (*a*) (i) Herbivore/(primary) consumer

(ii)

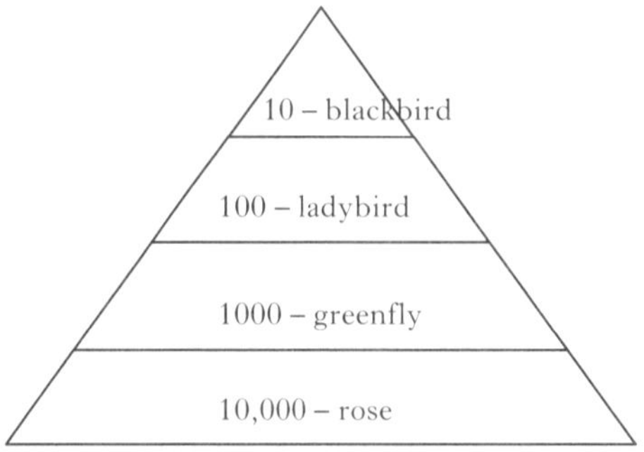

(iii) Used in/lost as heat/in movement/in waste /indigestible material/lost as waste product
or correct example

(*b*) They belong to the same/one species

6. (*a*) 11 : 1

(*b*) discontinuous

(*c*) (i) A and B

(ii) Both alleles are expressed equally in the phenotype **or**
Both are equal/dominant to each other **or**
Both in the phenotype

7. (*a*) (i) Zygote/fertilised (egg) cell

(ii) Q

(iii) **Double set** anther, R, embryo

Single set ovule

(*b*) Double set (of chromosomes) is restored when the zygote is formed/to restore chromosome number at fertilisation **or**
So offspring have a set (of chromosomes) from each parent
or
To allow two single sets to join in the zygote/ embryo at fertilisation

(*c*) Meiosis increases variation

8. (*a*) Temperature **or**
humidity/moisture/damp

(*b*) Woodlice spend most time in dark/least time in light/(most) woodlice move into the dark/out of the light

(*c*) Protects/Prevents them drying out
or escapes/hidden from predators
or increases chances of survival

9. (*a*) (i) Variation/difference in size and shape
or
Length and width/depth/height

(ii) (Availability of different types of) food/habitat/diet/prey/competition for food/habitat

(*b*) Niche

(*c*) (i) Deforestation/destruction of habitat/hunting/trapping/pollution/introduction of non-native species/tourism/forestry/farming

(ii) Decrease (due to extinction/dying out of species)

10. (*a*) (i) D C A B

(ii) A or B

(*b*)

	false	high
true		
	false	increases

11. *(a)* (i) B

(ii) Less protein in diet/more water intake/dilute urine/low ADH/toxic/poisonous
High Water Concentration in blood/urine
Kidney/liver damage/disease
Less deamination

(iii) (Litmus paper turns blue) more quickly/shorter times

(iv) (distilled) water in place of urine (sample)

(b) (i) glomerulus

(ii) Water/salts/glucose/some materials are absorbed into the blood /reabsorbed/absorbed from the filtrate

12. *(a)* D
bronchus/bronchi
air-sac/alveoli
A

(b) (i) 15
(ii) 3

13. *(a)* (i) Brain and spinal cord

(ii) Medulla

(b) (i) Sensory neurone/nerve **or** receptor

(ii) Pass nerve impulse/message/information (from sensory neurone) to motor neurone

(c) Reduces harm to the body/to move away from harmful stimuli **or**
Protect from danger/damage/harm **or**
Rapid/automatic/involuntary response to avoid harm/protect

SECTION C

1A
Maximum of three from:
P1 Chlorophyll/chloroplasts absorbs (energy of) light
P2 to split water into hydrogen and oxygen
P3 oxygen released
P4 ATP produced
P5 Light energy converted to chemical energy
P6 Hydrogen combines with a hydrogen acceptor
Maximum of three from:
C1 Carbon dioxide enters
C2 This stage is enzyme controlled
C3 ATP supplies the energy needed
C4 Hydrogen joins with Carbon dioxide
C5 Glucose/starch/cellulose is formed.

1B
Maximum of three from:
A1 Surrounding/Hypotonic solution has higher water concentration
A2 Water enters/fills (animal) cells/water diffuses into cells
A3 By osmosis/from HWC to LWC (or P3)
A4 Cells swell
A5 And burst
A6 Because no cell wall present
Maximum of three from:
P1 Surrounding/Hypertonic solution has lower water concentration
P2 Water leaves (plant) cells/water diffuses out of cells
P3 By osmosis/from HWC to LWC (or A3)
P4 Vacuole shrinks
P5 Cell membrane pulled away from cell wall/cell contents shrink
P6 Cell becomes plasmolysed/flaccid

2A
Maximum of three from:
Digestion
D1 Liver manufactures bile
D2 Bile emulsifies fats/forms smaller fat droplets/neutralises stomach contents/acids
D3 Pancreas produces digestive enzymes **or** named enzyme
Named enzyme plus substrate or product e.g.
D4 amylase breaks down starch
D5 lipase produces fatty acids and glycerol
D6 trypsin breaks down proteins/peptides

Maximum of three from:
Processing
P1 Glucose used in production of energy/ATP/respiration
P2 Glucose converted to glycogen in liver **or**
Vitamins/minerals stored in the liver
P3 Amino acids used in growth/repair/protein formation
P4 Excess amino acids deaminated in liver
P5 To form urea

2B
Maximum of one from:
Antibodies
A1 antibodies produced by lymphocytes
Maximum of two from:
A2 specific to antigen/bacteria/virus/foreign material/microbes
A3 combines/joins/fits with antigen/bacteria/virus/foreign material/microbes
A4 bacteria/virus/foreign material/microbes contain antigens
A5 destroys bacteria/virus/foreign material/microbes **or** agglutination

Maximum of one from:
Phagocytosis
P1 Phagocytosis carried out by macrophages/phagocytes/monocytes
Maximum of two from:
P2 Cell surrounds/engulfs antigen/bacteria/virus/foreign material/microbes
P3 Into a vesicle/vacuole
P4 Cell digests antigen/bacteria/virus/foreign material/microbes
P5 Using enzymes

BIOLOGY INTERMEDIATE 2 2010

SECTION A

1. B	11. B	21. D
2. A	12. D	22. B
3. C	13. B	23. C
4. B	14. C	24. A
5. D	15. A	25. D
6. B	16. C	
7. A	17. A	
8. D	18. C	
9. C	19. B	
10. A	20. D	

SECTION B

1. (*a*) (i) Controls entry and exit of materials
Contains genetic information **or** controls cell activities (specific activity must be correct) Cytoplasm

(ii) Q **and**
contains cell wall/vacuole

(*b*) (i) bacteria
lactose

(ii) Alcohol **and** petrol

(iii) To kill/destroy <u>bacteria</u> **or** prevent <u>bacterial</u> growth

2. (*a*) (i) Oxygen

(ii) Water

(iii) Add boiled liver instead

(iv) Measure volume/height of foam (in a given time)

(*b*) *Any two from:*
Concentration of hydrogen peroxide
Time left for
pH
Temperature of enzyme/tissue

(*c*) Active site/enzyme shape changes **or** substrate no longer fits

3. (*a*) 38

(*b*) Y → X

(*c*) **Name** Glycolysis
Product Pyruvic acid

4. (*a*) X light intensity
Y carbon dioxide concentration

(*b*) Number of bubbles/volume of oxygen produced per unit time
or CO2 uptake with time
or increase in dry mass with time

(*c*) (i) Chlorophyll/chloroplast

(ii) Used to split water **or** to form ATP **or** converted to <u>chemical</u> energy

(*d*) (i) Carbon fixation

(ii) Glucose

5. (*a*) More squid/food available for seals (to eat) or
Less competition for food

(*b*)

Statement	*True*	*False*	*Correction*
In this food web krill are <u>herbivores</u>		✓	Omnivores
The population of <u>sperm whales</u> has the highest biomass		✓	Plant plankton
The range of species in a <u>population</u> is called biodiversity		✓	Community/ Ecosystem/ habitat

6. (*a*) (i) WW (both caps/same size

(ii) Male gametes R, W (any order)
Offspring RW, RR (RW, RR)

(*b*) Polygenic

(*c*) Blood group – discontinous **and**
Height – continuous

(*d*) The effect of the environment on phenotype/ appearance

7. (*a*) 69

(*b*) Very low

(*c*) x-axis scale and label correct
y-axis scale correct
Three bars for **average times** plotted accurately
<u>both</u> axes must use at least 50% of graph paper provided

(*d*) As light intensity increases, time taken to travel 10cm decreases **or** vice versa

8. (*a*) (i) Prey **and** secondary

(ii) 64 (%)

(*b*) No effect **and** no <u>species</u> becomes extinct
or
Decrease **and** <u>species</u> become extinct/number of species decreases

(*c*) Sewage/fertilizers/industry/oil/acid rain

9. (*a*) P (salivary) amylase
Q pepsin

(*b*) Muscles behind food contract **and** in front of food relax (1)
Food is pushed (down the small intestine) (1)

(*c*) *Any two from:*
Increased surface area/villi/long/folded (1)
Thin (gut) wall/lining (1)
Good blood supply (1)

10. (*a*) (i) P arrow towards lungs **and**
Q arrow towards the body

(ii) P deoxygenated **and**
Q oxygenated

(*b*) S <u>left</u> atrium
R pulmonary <u>vein</u>

(*c*) To stop backflow <u>of blood</u>

(*d*) Reduces blood (flow)/glucose/oxygen to heart muscle

11. (*a*) Y filtration more

(*b*) Liver

(*c*) Osmoregulation

12. (*a*) Alcohol increases (average) reaction times

(*b*) To reduce effect of rogue results/to improve reliability of results

(*c*) 50 (%)

(*d*) Cerebellum

SECTION C

1A

Maximum of two from:

L1 Air/oxygen breathed in through trachea/windpipe/ nose/mouth
L2 Air/oxygen passes down through bronchi/ bronchioles
L3 Air/oxygen moves into alveolus/air sac
L4 Oxygen dissolves/diffuses through (moist) lining/wall

Maximum of two from:

B1 Into red blood cell
B2 Into capillary/blood/forms oxygenated blood
B3 Joins to haemoglobin/forms oxyhaemoglobin
B4 Blood taken to heart (via pulmonary vein)

Maximum of two from:

S1 From heart via aorta/arteries
S2 Carried to skin (cells)
S3 Oxyhaemoglobin gives up oxygen to (skin) cells/oxygen passes into cells

D Higher oxygen concentration to lower oxygen concentration (can be awarded only once in section L **or** S)

1B

Maximum of two from:

C1 Act as energy store
C2 Provide energy (via respiration)
C3 Contain C, H and O (or full names)
C4 Simple sugars/glucose

Maximum of two from:

F1 Insulation energy store/provides energy
F2 Contain C, H and O
F3 Fatty acids
F4 Glycerol

Maximum of two from:

P1 Growth/repair
P2 Contain C, H, O and N
P3 Amino acids

2A

Maximum of three from:

Adaptions

A1 Roots – long/deep
A2 Superficial/shallow/under surface roots
A3 Small leaves/no leaves/spines/needles/thorns/spikes
A4 Thick waxy cuticle (on leaves) (not skin)
A5 Succulent tissue/any other correct desert adaptation

Maximum of three from:

Explanations – must relate to the correct point above

E1 (Increases chance of) absorbing water from deep soil (for A1)
E2 (Increases chance of) absorbing surface water (for A2)
E3 Decreases/reduces water loss (for A3 or A4)
E4 Protects plant from animals (for A3)
E5 Stores water (for A5)/any other correct explanation to match A5

2B

Maximum of three from:

Differences body cells and gametes

D1 Zygote/body cells (or named examples) have double sets/diploid/pairs of chromosomes
D2 Gametes have single set/haploid/half the parent cell chromosome number
D3 Zygote/body cells have 46/23 pairs of chromosomes
D4 Gametes have 23 chromosomes

Maximum of three from:

Sex determination

S1 Male gametes/sperm contain X or Y chromosome
S2 Female gametes/eggs contain an X chromosome
S3 At fertilisation the zygote is formed **or** at fertilisation the gametes fuse
S4 XX – Female (human) **or** XY – Male (human)
S5 Sperm/male gamete determine the sex of (human) offspring

BIOLOGY INTERMEDIATE 2 2011

SECTION A

1. D	11. B	21. C
2. B	12. C	22. D
3. C	13. A	23. A
4. D	14. A	24. B
5. A	15. C	25. A
6. D	16. C	
7. B	17. A	
8. C	18. D	
9. B	19. B	
10. D	20. B	

SECTION B

1. (*a*) (i) X = (sap) vacuole
Y = cytoplasm

(ii) stores genetic information/DNA/chromosomes
controls cell activity(ies)/function(s)

(*b*) (potato/starch) phosphorylase

(*c*) D = only plants have a cell wall/chloroplast/vacuole
S = both have membranes/cytoplasm/nuclei

2. (*a*) fungi carbon dioxide gasohol

(*b*) (bacteria) convert <u>lactose to lactic acid</u>
lactic acid clots milk/causes curdling

3. (*a*) (i) X and Y axes labels and units correct (as table)
(ii) Correct plot and join of all points

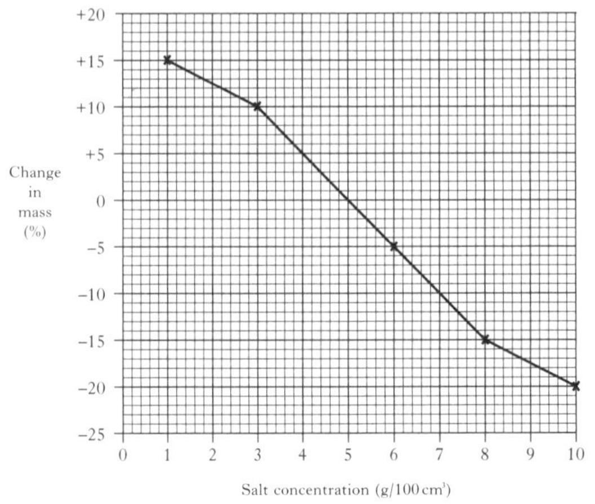

(*b*) *Any two from:*
type/size/number of potato/cylinders
type/pH/volume of (salt) <u>solution</u>
temperature

(*c*) 5 [or where graph line crosses X axis]
no change in <u>mass/weight</u>

(*d*) 7 [or correct value from graph]

4. (*a*) enzyme has an active site

enzyme/active site is complementary/matching shape/specific to substrate

(*b*) denatured/
changes <u>shape</u>/
reduced activity

(*c*) pH **or** concentration of enzyme/substrate

(*d*) water and oxygen

5. (*a*) habitat/holt

(*b*) less shelter/place to live/habitat/breeding ground/food available
(more chance of being) seen by predators/prey
increased competition for habitat

(*c*) otter numbers would decrease
(otters and mink) in competition for food/fish/habitat

(*d*) producer

eats animals <u>only</u>

<u>all</u> the plants and animals/
populations/
species/
organisms/
living things

6. (*a*) 320

(*b*) 50% (increase) / 33% / 33.3% (decrease)

(*c*) (i) (pheno) type/variety of cotton/
plant resistant or not

(ii) to compare mass/yields/
to show any difference in mass/yields is due to variety of cotton

(iii) improve/increase reliability of <u>results</u>

(*d*) R cotton produces a higher yield (than V cotton)

(*e*) (i) It is resistant to the boll weevil/insects

(ii) Less pesticide so fewer insects die

7. (*a*) (i) HH, hh
(ii) Wavy
(iii) Hh

(*b*) co-dominant

(*c*) order, bases, protein

8. (*a*) stomach and <u>small</u> intestine

(*b*) (i) 2000
(ii) 67/66·7

9. (*a*) it increases then decreases
maximum/optimum/highest/change at <u>pH8</u>

(*b*) depth of clear jelly will be less than 2 mm/any value less than 2mm

(*c*) *Any two from:*
lipase
amylase
peptidase

10. (*a*) hypotonic excreting concentrated

(*b*) (i) Q = Bowman's capsule
(ii) (ultra)filtration

(*c*) (i) pituitary gland
(ii) Tubule/collecting duct/loop of Henle

11. (*a*) True
False speed up
False carbon dioxide

(*b*) (as) oxyhaemoglobin/(on) haemoglobin

(*c*) *Any two from:*
carbon dioxide/sugars/glucose/amino acids/proteins/fats/vitamins/urea/hormones/salts/water/oxygen/antibodies/platelets

12. (*a*) *Any three from:*

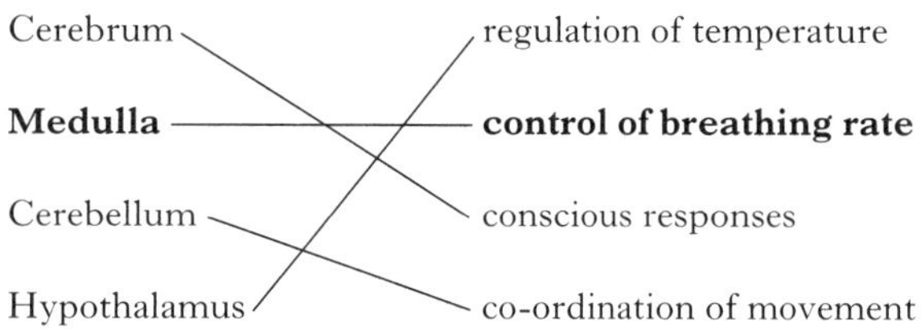

(*b*) (i) 1. sensory
2. relay/association/interneurone
3. motor

(ii) provides a rapid response/protects the body (from harm)/prevent further damage

SECTION C

1A

N1 X is a pyramid of numbers

Maximum of two from:

N2 oak tree few/one
N3 caterpillar more numerous than oak
N4 any correct number relationship between hawk and thrush **or** caterpillar and thrush
N5 numbers decrease moving along the food chain (caterpillar to hawk)
N6 any correct description of 'block' sizes

Maximum of two from:

E1 oak tree has highest energy
E2 correct position of any organism in the pyramid
E3 caterpillar/thrush/hawk level has less energy than any level below
E4 energy used/decreases/lost at each stage
E5 (energy lost by) movement/heat/waste products (or any other correct)
E6 any correct description of 'block' sizes

1B

M1 Cell A sperm/**male** gamete/**male** sex cell

Maximum of two from:

M2 (matching/homologous) chromosomes pair **or** random assortment
M3 produces variation
M4 double set/2 sets/diploid/46 chromosomes
M5 pairs separate
M6 gametes/sex cell 1 set/haploid/23/ half the number of chromosomes
M7 four gametes/sex cells produced

Maximum of two from:

F1 gametes/sex cells fuse
F2 any correct description of fusion of gamete/sex cell nuclei (*must indicate male/female*)
F3 to form a zygote
F4 this is a random process
F5 produces variation
F6 X sperm produce female offspring/Y sperm produce male offspring
F7 zygote contains/restores 2 sets/diploid/46 chromosomes

2A

Maximum of three from:

G1 overall equation [*not under stage 1*]
G2 **first stage** is glycolysis
G3 enzyme controlled
G4 glucose is broken down/used/raw material
G5 pyruvic acid is produced
G6 **2** ATP produced
G7 anaerobic stage/no oxygen needed

Maximum of three from:

K1 second stage enzyme controlled
K2 pyruvic acid used/raw material
K3 oxygen used/raw material
K4 36 ATP produced/total 38 ATP produced
K5 carbon dioxide and water produced

2B

Maximum of three from:

P1 overall equation [including light and chlorophyll] [*not under stage 1*]
P2 **first stage** is photolysis/light reaction
P3 enzyme controlled
P4 light energy trapped by chlorophyll
P5 water is broken down/used/raw material
P6 oxygen is released/produced
P7 ATP/hydrogen is produced
P8 ATP/hydrogen is passed to second stage

Maximum of three from:

C1 **second stage** is carbon fixation/Calvin's cycle/light independent reaction
C2 enzyme controlled
C3 carbon dioxide is used/raw material
C4 ATP provides energy/hydrogen used
C5 hydrogen added to carbon dioxide
C6 glucose is produced

BrightRED PUBLISHING

Published by Bright Red Publishing Ltd, 6 Stafford Street, Edinburgh, EH3 7AU
Tel: 0131 220 5804, Fax: 0131 220 6710, enquiries: sales@brightredpublishing.co.uk,
www.brightredpublishing.co.uk

Official SQA answers to 978-1-84948-194-6
2007-2011